The lyric baritone

Reimar Hüsch Metternich
Uhde Wächter

With valuable assistance from Clifford Elkin

Discographies compiled
by John Hunt

The Lyric Baritone
Published by John Hunt.
Designed by Richard Chlupaty
© 1997 John Hunt
reprinted 2009
ISBN 9780952582-78-6

Published 1997 by John Hunt
Designed by Richard Chlupaty, London

Copyright 1997 John Hunt

Sole distributors:
Travis & Emery,
17 Cecil Court,
London, WC2N 4EZ,
United Kingdom.
(+44) 20 7 459 2129.
sales@travis-and-emery.com

CONTENTS

3   Acknowledgement
4   Introduction
7   Hans Reinmar discography
29 Gerhard Hüsch discography
115 Josef Metternich discography
153 Hermann Uhde discography
175 Eberhard Wächter discography
220 Credits

ACKNOWLEDGEMENT

This publication has been made possible by contributions and advance subscriptions from the following

Richard Ames, New Barnet
Stefano Angeloni, Frasso Sabino
Yoshihiro Asada, Osaka
Jack Atkinson, Tasmania
Bruno Barthelmé, Le Creusot
E.C. Blake, York
J. Camps-Ros, Barcelona
J. Charrington, Cardiff
Eduardo Chibas, Caracas
Robert Christoforides, Fordingbridge
A. Copeman, Cambridge
F. De Vilder, Bussum
Richard Dennis, Greenhithe
John Derry, Newcastle-upon-Tyne
Hans-Peter Ebner, Milan
Bill Flowers, London
Henry Fogel, Chicago
T. Foley, Cork
Peter Fu, Hong Kong
Nobuo Fukumoto, Hamamatsu
Peter Fulop, Toronto
James Giles, Sidcup
Philip Goodman, London
Jean-Pierre Goossens, Luxembourg
Johann Gratz, Vienna
Peter Hammann, Bochum
Michael Harris, London
Tadashi Hasegawa, Nagoya
Naoya Hirabayashi, Tokyo
Martin Holland, Sale
John Hughes, Brisbane
Bodo Igesz, New York
Richard Igler, Vienna
Eugene Kaskey, New York
Shiro Kawai, Tokyo

Rodney Kempster, Basingstoke
Detlef Kissmann, Solingen
Eric Kobe, Lucerne
Elisabeth Legge-Schwarzkopf DBE, Zürich
John Mallinson, Hurst Green
Carlo Marinelli, Rome
Finn Moeller Larsen, Virum
Philip Moores, Stafford
Bruce Morrison, Gillingham
W. Moyle, Ombersley
Alan Newcombe, Hamburg
Hugh Palmer, Chelmsford
Jim Parsons, Sutton Coldfield
Laurence Pateman, London
James Pearson, Vienna
Tully Potter, Billericay
Peter Pugson, Buxton
Phil Rees, Pewsey
Patrick Russell, Calstock
Yves Saillard, Mollie-Margot
T. Scanes, Ashford
Neville Sumpter, Northolt
Yoshihiko Suzuki, Tokyo
H.A. Van Dijk, Apeldoorn
Mario Vicentini, Cassano Magnano
Hiromitsu Wada, Chiba
Urs Weber, St Gallen
G. Wright, Romford
Ken Wyman, Brentwood
Masakasu Abe, Chiba City
Helger Steinhauff, Stemwede
John Larsen, Mariager
Valery Ryvkin, New York

THE LYRIC BARITONE

Categorisation of the singing voice yields at best the most approximate of indications as to type and quality of the singer concerned. At what point, for example, does the lyric soprano take on characteristics of the spinto or again, when does a Wagnerian Heldenbariton assume the qualities of a true black bass?

In the case of the five baritones of German schooling whose recordings are catalogued in this volume - and I must immediately state that the choice is my own subjective one - I have come across the description "character baritone" being used by more than one expert in the field. I take this to mean, in these particular cases, that the voice possesses a lightness and clarity which embraces youthfulness as well as maturity, legato smoothness as well as assertiveness.

The choice, or grouping, as has often happened in my previous volumes of singer discographies, takes in the pre-war era, from the very outset of electric recording in the mid 1920s (singers, therefore, whom most of us can have known only from recordings) but also crosses into the modern, or post-war, period to include one or more example of a singer who is no longer performing but who, in the role of teacher, has been active in passing on some of his wisdom to todays's young practitioners. This certainly applies to Josef Metternich and Eberhard Wächter, who until his death in 1988 served as mentor to one of today's young hopefuls in the field of lyric baritones, the Dane Bo Skovhus (Wächter's discography included here is of course an up-date of the one which I included in my 1992 volume "More Viennese singers").

The repertoire for our baritones contains many interesting parallels and overlaps, and the recorded examples in most cases reflect those operatic parts they performed during their stage careers. Roles which feature frequently here include Mozart's Count, Giovanni, Figaro and Guglielmo (Papageno also, in the case of Gerhard Hüsch), Gounod's Valentin, Weber's Ottokar, Humperdinck's Besenbinder and Spielmann, Bizet's Escamillo, Wagner's Wolfram and Amfortas (extending, in the cases of Reinmar and Uhde, to Wotan), Strauss' Mandryka, Verdi's Rigoletto, Renato, Luna, Amonasro and Iago, Rossini's Barber, Offenbach's Dapertutto and Tchaikovsky's Onegin.

Hans Reinmar, was a great favourite at Berlin's Städtische Oper (and also Staatsoper, in a brief post-war period of activity), and a Preiser CD (89112) illustrates, in a cross-section of his repertoire, his very seductive and virile timbre. Another Preiser CD (90271) gives us a glimpse, in a war-time radio recording, of Reinmar's accomplished Verdi singing (Otello extracts with Helge Rosvaenge).

The reputation of **Gerhard Hüsch** as the first modern Lieder singer has perhaps lessened our awareness of him as an operatic baritone of high calibre (performing the role of Wolfram in "Tannhäuser" under Toscanini at Bayreuth, but not in the subsequent HMV records conducted by Elmendorff). CDs from Pearl and Preiser afford the modern listener the chance of appreciating Hüsch's achievement.

Starting his career in the dark latter years of the Third Reich, it is all the more remarkable that **Josef Metternich** should have found acceptance, both in German and Italian roles, at New York's Metropolitan in the 1950s. He is probably the most accomplished Italian stylist amongst our five German/Austrian baritones. Excerpts from his Italian repertoire were performed, albeit in German, for Electrola's microphones, whereas only one extant recording (Verdi's "Ballo in maschera" from the Met) lets us hear him actually singing in Italian.

The particular nobility tinged with anguish which characterises the timbre of **Hermann Uhde** marked him out as a near-ideal interpreter of Wagner roles such as the Dutchman, Amfortas and Gunther, although a darker malevolence was evoked in his portrayals of Telramund and Klingsor. Outside the Wagnerian sphere, Uhde seems to have been under-employed by recording companies, but fortunately he took part in many broadcasts which have subsequently been transferred to disc.

Like Uhde, **Eberhard Wächter** died early, although he had spent more time in opera administration than in singing in his later years. Although mainly an opera singer, Wächter also made a select number of Lieder recordings, Beethoven and Wolf for Deutsche Grammophon and Schumann for Decca (with Alfred Brendel). His contributions to Italian opera (mainly on Eurodisc LPs) are perhaps less special: it is Wächter's Wolfram and Amfortas, not to mention his Don Giovanni (in my opinion still underrated), which earn him a place in the line of great modern baritones on record.

The discographies are arranged chronologically by composer and are set out in three columns: first column gives place, month and year in which the recording took place; second column gives other participating soloists, orchestra and conductor or accompanying pianist; third column contains the catalogue issue numbers (first issues, subsequent editions in the most important territories in the formats of 78, 45, LP and CD). Selected unpublished tapes, mainly from radio transmissions, are included in the hope that they might still be located and found worthy of publication.

A word about the opera **Querschnitte** or highlights which were particularly popular in Germany during the LP era, but which already existed in the days of 78s, when a disc would contain mere sections from arias or ensembles joined together either by the conductor or technicians to form a potpourri. The actual contents of the 78 disc was not necessarily listed on the label. It should be borne in mind, and this also applies to LP highlights, that alternative recordings of individual arias by the same artist may exist within such a **Querschnitt** or highlights compilation. It should also be noted that excerpt discs from complete opera recordings are only listed if they contain a contribution from the artist under examination.

Lieder are listed individually in most cases, with an indication of the cycle from which they may be drawn, where necessary.

I am always glad to hear from readers who can furnish me with additional catalogue numbers or any other information relating to the recordings. A list of those who have helped with information so far can be found at the back of this volume, although I must single out here the invaluable assistance I have obtained from the Clifford Elkin collection in those frequent cases where I myself could not locate a copy of a particular recording.

John Hunt 1997

Hans Reinmar
1895-1961

Discography compiled
by John Hunt

FRANZ ABT (1819-1885)

Wenn man beim Wein sitzt Soldatenart

Berlin March 1935	BPO Schmidt-Isserstedt	78: Telefunken E 1832 LP: Preiser LV 83 CD: Preiser 89112

GEORGES BIZET (1838-1875)

Carmen, excerpt (Votre toast)

Berlin September 1927	Staatskapelle Weissmann <u>Sung in German</u>	78: Odeon O-11747 LP: Preiser LV 83
Berlin May 1928	Staatskapelle Weigert <u>Sung in German</u>	LP: Preiser LV 1347 CD: Preiser 89112

JOHANNES BRAHMS (1833-1897)

An die Leier

Berlin   Unnamed pianist   78: Odeon O-6518
November 1926   LP: Preiser LV 1347

Wie bist du, meine Königin?

Berlin   Unnamed pianist   78: Odeon O-6518
November 1926   LP: Preiser LV 1347

4 Zigeunerlieder: Zigeuner, greifet in die Saiten!; Hochgetürmte Rimaflut; Kommt dir manchmal in den Sinn; Brauner Bursche führt zum Tanze

Berlin   Unnamed pianist   LP: Preiser LV 1347
November 1926

GAETONO DONIZETTI (1797-1848)

Lucia di Lammermoor, excerpt (Chi mi frema)

Berlin 1941	Piltti, Schilp, Rosvaenge, Zimmermann, Lang Städtische Oper Orchestra Rother <u>Sung in German</u>	LP: BASF KBF 21485

ENGLELBERT HUMPERDINCK (1854-1921)

Königskinder, excerpt (Verdorben, gestorben!)

Berlin February 1934	BPO Reuss	78: Telefunken E 1657 LP: Telefunken GMA 57 LP: Preiser LV 83 CD: Preiser 89112

RUGGIERO LEONCAVALLO (1858-1918)

I pagliacci, excerpt (Si può?)

Berlin 1942-1943	Orchestra Steinkopf <u>Sung in German</u>	Unpublished radio broadcast

DEUTSCHES  OPERNHAUS
BERLIN

Sonnabend, den 17. Januar 1942 • Runde I

Gaſtſpiel des italieniſchen Dirigenten Mario Roſſi
unter ſeiner muſikaliſchen Einſtudierung und Leitung

In der Neuinſzenierung

Othello

Oper in 4 Akten von Giuſeppe Verdi
Text von Arrigo Boito, deutſch von Max Kalbeck

Inſzenierung: Gotthelf Piſtor
Bühnenbilder und Koſtüme: Paul Haſerung

Anfang 17.30 Uhr   Ende 20.30 Uhr

Personenverzeichnis:

Othello, Mohr, Befehlshaber der venezianischen Flotte	August Seider a. G.
Jago, Fähnrich	Hans Reinmar
Cassio, Hauptmann	Willi Wörle
Rodrigo, ein edler Venezianer	Rudolf Schramm
Lodovico, Gesandter der Republik Venedig	Wilhelm Lang
Montano, Vorgänger Othellos in der Statthalterei von Cypern	Edwin Heyer
Ein Herold	Josef Metternich
Desdemona, Othellos Gattin	Constanze Nettesheim
Emilia, Jagos Gattin	Emmi Hagemann

Soldaten und Seeleute der Republik Venedig, Edeldamen und venezianische Nobili, Cyprioten, griechische, dalmatinische und albanesische Krieger, Volk usw.

Ort der Handlung: Eine Hafenstadt der Insel Cypern

Zeit: Ende des fünfzehnten Jahrhunderts

Chöre: Hermann Lüddecke   Technische Leitung: Kurt Hemmerling

Keine Ouvertüre

Größere Pause nach dem 1. und 2. Akt, kleinere nach dem 3. Akt

---

Bei Fliegeralarm: Den Anordnungen der Logenschließer ist unbedingt Folge zu leisten; die Garderoben bleiben geschlossen; Kleidungsstücke werden nicht ausgehändigt.

HEINRICH MARSCHNER (1795-1861)

Hans Heiling, excerpt (An jenem Tag)

Berlin	BPO	78: Telefunken E 1657
February 1934	Reuss	LP: Telefunken GMA 57
		LP: Preiser LV 83
		CD: Preiser 89112

GIACOMO MEYERBEER (1791-1864)

L'Africaine, excerpt (Fille des rois!)

Berlin	Staatskapelle	78: Odeon O-6599
September 1927	Weissmann	LP: Preiser LV 83
	Sung in German	CD: Preiser 89112

L'Africaine, excerpt (Adamastor, roi des vagues!)

Berlin	Staatskapelle	LP: Preiser LV 1347
May 1928	Weigert	CD: Preiser 89112
	Sung in German	

MODEST MOUSSORGSKY (1839-1881)

Song of the flea

Berlin	Unnamed	78: Odeon O-28111
1927	accompaniment	
	Sung in German	

WOLFGANG AMADEUS MOZART (1756-1791)

Don Giovanni, excerpt (Fin ch' han dal vino)

Berlin	Staatskapelle	LP: Preiser LV 1347
April 1928	Weigert	CD: Preiser 89112
	Sung in German	

Don Giovanni, excerpt (Deh vieni alla finestra)

Berlin	Staatskapelle	LP: Preiser LV 1347
April 1928	Weigert	CD: Preiser 89112
	Sung in German	

Don Giovanni, excerpt (Là ci darem la mano)

Berlin	Eisinger	78: Ultraphon A 401
1930	Städtische Oper	LP: Discophilia DIS 13
	Orchestra	LP: Preiser LV 197
	Zweig	
	Sung in German	

VIKTOR NESSLER (1841-1890)

Der Trompeter von Säckingen, excerpt (Behüt' dich Gott!)

Berlin	BPO	78: Telefunken E 1832
March 1935	Schmidt-Isserstedt	CD: Preiser 89112

16 Reinmar

JACQUES OFFENBACH (1819-1880)

Les contes d'Hoffmann, excerpt (Scintille diamant!)

Berlin	Staatskapelle	78: Odeon O-6600
September 1927	Weissmann	LP: Preiser LV 83
	<u>Sung in German</u>	CD: Preiser 89112

GIACOMO PUCCINI (1858-1924)

La Bohème, excerpt (O Mimì, tu più non torni!)

Berlin	Wittrisch	78: Telefunken E 1756
April 1934	BPO	
	Reuss	
	<u>Sung in German</u>	

Gianni Schicchi

Cologne	<u>Role of Schicchi</u>	Unpublished radio broadcast
November	Rau, R.Fischer,	
1949	Werkenmeier,	
	Schirp	
	WDR Orchestra	
	and Chorus	
	Kraus	
	<u>Sung in German</u>	

Il tabarro

Cologne	<u>Role of Marcel</u>	Unpublished radio broadcast
November	Hoffmann-Parrels,	
1949	Bajew	
	WDR Orchestra	
	Kraus	
	<u>Sung in German</u>	

JOHANN STRAUSS (1825-1899)

Die Fledermaus

Berlin August 1936	Role of Frank Eipperle, Beilke, Fidesser, Hüsch, Marischka Reichssender Orchestra & Chorus Hainisch	Unpublished radio broadcast

Die Fledermaus, unspecified extracts

Berlin February 1934	Role of Frank Berger, Pfahl, Heindl, Wörle Hüsch Staatskapelle and Chorus Müller	Unpublished radio broadcast Tapes probably destroyed

RICHARD STRAUSS (1864-1949)

Arabella

Salzburg August 1942	Role of Mandryka Ursuleac, Eipperle, Böttcher, Willer, Taubmann, Klarwein, T.Herrmann Vienna Opera Chorus VPO Krauss	CD: Myto MCD 92154

PIOTR TCHAIKOVSKY (1840-1893)

Evgeny Onegin excerpts (You have written to me; Can it really be that same Tatiana?)

Berlin February 1926	Staatskapelle Weigert Sung in German	LP: Preiser LV 1347

WEIN — HAUS — HUTH
WEINGROSSHANDLUNG
WEINSTUBEN

BERLIN W 9
POTSDAMER STRASSE 139
ECKE LINKSTR. / NAHE PLATZ

Turnus III

Sonnabend, den 1. März 1930

MIGNON

Oper in 3 Akten (4 Bildern)
Text nach Goethes „Wilhelm Meister" von M. Carré und J. Barbier
Musik von Ambroise Thomas
Musikalische Leitung: Dr. Fritz Stiedry. Inszenierung: Otto Krauß
Bühnenbilder: Emil Preetorius
(Aus dem Fundus neu zusammengestellt)

Kassenöffnung 18½ (6½) Uhr Anfang 19½ (7½) Uhr
Ende 22½ (10½) Uhr

Eigener Untergrundbahnhof mit direktem Eingang zur Städtischen Oper

Wilhelm Meister	Koloman Pataky a. G.
Mignon	Maria Ivogün
Philine	Marguerite Perras
Laertes	Edwin Heyer
Lothario	Hans Reinmar
Friedrich	Harry Steier
Jarno, Führer einer Zigeunerbande	Paul Seebach
Der Fürst	Fritz Hartel
Die Fürstin	Luise Scholl
Baron Rosenberg	Erich Streubel
Antonio	Wilhelm Spering
Eine Zofe	Hedwig Höpfner
Zafarie	Artur Halwas
Ein Diener des Barons	Carl Roeber
Ein Souffleur	Fritz Kraft
Der Wirt	Paul Struensee

Damen und Herren vom Hofe, Schauspieler und Schauspielerinnen, Zigeuner und Zigeunerinnen, Diener, Dienerinnen, Reisende, Bürger, Bürgerinnen

Nach der Vorstellung
ZU LUTTER & WEGNER
ins
OPERNRESTAURANT
Direkter Zugang durch das Parterre-Foyer

IM STÄDT. OPERNHAUS

Bier und Wein in allen Abteilungen, kein Weinzwang
Vorzügliche Küche zu soliden Preisen

GIUSEPPE VERDI (1813-1901)

Aida, excerpt (Ciel! Mio padre!)

Munich May 1949	Kupper Bavarian State Orchestra Solti Sung in German	LP: DG LPEM 19 027

Aida, excerpt (Gloria all' Egitto!)

Berlin June 1932	Yoder, Kindermann, Graveur, Sande Staatskapelle and Chorus Meyrowitz Sung in German	78: Telefunken F 1161 LP: Historia H 647

Un ballo in maschera, excerpt (Eri tu)

Berlin February 1926	Staatskapelle Weigert Sung in German	LP: Preiser LV 1347
Berlin June 1932	BPO Meyrowitz Sung in German	78: Telefunken F 1160 LP: Telefunken GMA 57 LP: Preiser LV 83 CD: Preiser 89112

Don Carlo, excerpt (Per me giunto è il di supremo)

Berlin September 1927	Städtische Oper Orchestra Borchert Sung in German	78: Telefunken E 1494 LP: Telefunken GMA 57 LP: Preiser LV 83 CD: Preiser 89112

Falstaff

Cologne April 1950	Role of Falstaff Cunitz, Lipp, R.Fischer,Lasser, Holm, Peter WDR Orchestra and Chorus Solti Sung in German	Unpublished radio broadcast

La forza del destino, excerpt (Solenne in quest' ora)

Berlin 1931	Wittrisch <u>Sung in German</u>	LP: Historia H 663-664

Otello, excerpt (Credo in un dio crudel)

Berlin September 1927	Staatskapelle Weissmann <u>Sung in German</u>	78: Odeon O-6599 LP: Preiser LV 83 CD: Preiser 89112
Berlin 1942-1943	Staatskapelle Steinkopf <u>Sung in German</u>	CD: Preiser 90271

Otello, excerpt (Desdemona rea!)

Berlin 1942-1943	Rosvaenge Staatskapelle Steinkopf <u>Sung in German</u>	CD: Preiser 90271

Otello, excerpt (Era la notte)

Berlin September 1933	Wittrisch BPO Reuss <u>Sung in German</u>	78: Telefunken E 1476 LP: Telefunken GMA 57 CD: Preiser 89112
Berlin 1942-1943	Rosvaenge Staatskapelle Steinkopf <u>Sung in German</u>	LP: Historia H 696-697 CD: Preiser 90271

Otello, excerpt (Sì per ciel!)

Berlin September 1933	Wittrisch BPO Reuss <u>Sung in German</u>	78: Telefunken E 1476 LP: Telefunken GMA 57 CD: Preiser 89112
Berlin 1942-1943	Rosvaenge Staatskapelle Steinkopf <u>Sung in German</u>	LP: Historis H 696-697 CD: Preiser 90271

Rigoletto, Querschnitt

Berlin October 1933	Anders, Bischoff, Ruziczka Städtische Oper Orchestra & Chorus Reuss Sung in German	78: Telefunken E 1509 LP: Preiser LV 83 Abridged versions of Pari siamo and Cortigiani

Rigoletto, excerpt (Bella figlia dell' amore)

Berlin June 1932	Yoder, Kindermann, Rosvaenge Staatskapelle Meyrowitz Sung in German	LP: Telefunken HT 24/AJ 642.084 LP: Preiser LV 515

Simon Boccanegra

Cologne July 1949	Role of Boccanegra E.Dietrich, Bajew, Fehn, Blasius, Wilhelms WDR Orchestra and Chorus Romansky Sung in German	Unpublished radio broadcast

Simon Boccanegra, excerpt (Plebe! Patrizi!)

Berlin June 1932	BPO Meyrowitz Sung in German	78: Telefunken F 1160 LP: Telefunken GMA 57 LP: Preiser LV 83 CD: Preiser 89112

La traviata, excerpt (Di provenza al mar)

Berlin September 1927	Staatskapelle Weissmann Sung in German	78: Odeon O-11747 LP: Preiser LV 83

Il trovatore, excerpt (Il balen del suo sorriso)

Berlin November 1925	Staatskapelle Weigert Sung in German	LP: Preiser LV 1347

RICHARD WAGNER (1813-1883)

Die Meistersinger von Nürnberg, excerpt (Selig wie die Sonne)

Berlin	Yoder, Kindermann,	78: Telefunken SK 1162
June 1932	Rosvaenge, Kuttner	LP: Telefunken HT 24/642 084AJ
	Staatskapelle	LP: Preiser LV 515
	Meyrowitz	LP: Top Classic TC 9042
		CD: Grammofono AB 78668-78669

Die Meistersinger von Nürnberg, excerpt (Wach auf!/Euch macht Ihr's leicht/ Verachtet mir die Meister nicht!)

Berlin	Städtische Oper	78: Telefunken E 1609
February 1934	Chorus	LP: Telefunken GMA 57
	BPO	
	Reuss	

Parsifal, Act 3

Berlin	Role of Amfortas	LP: Acanta DE 23.036
March 1942	Larcen, Hartmann,	CD: Acanta 44.2101-44.2102
	Weber	CD: Preiser 90261
	Städtische Oper	CD: Grammofono AB 78555
	Orchestra & Chorus	Excerpts
	Knappertsbusch	LP: Acanta HB 22.8630/40.23502
		Some editions incorrectly dated 1943

Tannhäuser, excerpt (Als du in kühnem Sange)

Berlin	Staatskapelle	78: Odeon 0-6569
September 1927	Weissmann	LP: Preiser LV 1347
		CD: Preiser 89112

Tannhäuser, excerpt (Blick' ich umher in diesem edlen Kreise)

Berlin	Staatskapelle	78: Odeon 0-6569
September 1927	Weissmann	LP: Preiser LV 1347
		LP: EMI 1C 181 30669-30678M
		CD: Preiser 89112

Tannhäuser, excerpt (O du mein holder Abendstern)

Berlin	Staatskapelle	78: Odeon 0-6332
April 1928	Weigert	LP: Preiser LV 1347
		CD: Preiser 89112

Städtisches Opernhaus

Mittwoch, den 28. September 1932

In neuer Einstudierung und Inszenierung zum 1. Male

EIN MASKENBALL

Oper in 3 Akten (6 Bildern) von F. M. Piave
Musik von Giuseppe Verdi
Musikalische Leitung: Fritz Busch a. G.
Inszenierung: Carl Ebert   Bühnenbild: Caspar Neher

Graf Richard, Gouverneur .... Koloman v. Pataky
René .... Hans Reinmar
Amelia, Renés Gattin .... Maria Németh
Ulrica, eine Wahrsagerin .... Sigrid Onégin
Oscar, Page des Grafen .... Erna Berger
Silvano, ein Matrose .... Rudolf Gonszar
Samuel ⎫ Verschworene .... Fred Destal
Tom   ⎭ .... Gotthold Ditter
Ein Richter .... Wilhelm Guttmann
Ein Diener .... Thorkild Noval

Chöre: Hermann Lüddecke

Choreographie: Lizzie Maudrik

Technische Leitung:
Maschineriedirektor Kurt Hemmerling

Im 6. Bild: Menuett:
  Damen: Abramowitsch, Sydow, Uhlen
  Herren: Egenlauf, Frank, Groke
Masken:
  Damen: Hettwer, Hirth, M. u. H. Höpfner, Juré, Kubbe, Lindner, Mewal
  Herren: Egenlauf, Jäger, Kamaroff, Otto, Sorge, Wois

Große Pause nach dem 3. Bild

Inhaltsangabe umseitig

Bayer. Staatstheater
Staatsoper Prinzregententheater

München, Samstag, 16. März 1946

Oper in vier Akten

Text von Arrigo Boito, für die deutsche Bühne übertragen von Max Kalbeck

Musik von Giuseppe Verdi

Musikalische Leitung: *Bertil Wetzelsberger*   Inszenierung und Bühnenbild: *Günther Rennert*

Othello, Mohr, Befehlshaber der venetianischen Flotte . . . *Franz Völker*
Jago, Fähnrich . . . . *Hans Reinmar*
Cassio, Hauptmann . . . . *Franz Klarwein*
Rodrigo, ein edler Venetianer . . . . *Heinz Braun-Buran*
Lodovico, Gesandter der Republik Venedig . . . . . . *Georg Wieter*
Montano, der Vorgänger Othellos in der Statthalterei von Cypern *Karl Schmidt*
Ein Herold . . . . *Friedrich Rauch*
Desdemona, Othellos Gemahlin . . . . *Maud Cunitz*
Emilia, Jagos Gattin . . . . *Irmgard Barth*

Soldaten und Seeleute der Republik Venedig, venetianische Nobili, Volk aus Cypern

Chor und Ballett der Staatsoper

Ort der Handlung: Eine Hafenstadt der Insel Cypern
Zeit: Ende des fünfzehnten Jahrhunderts

Chöre: *Herbert Erlenwein*

Feuertanz im 1. Akt: *Franziska Tona*, Ballettpantomime im 2. Akt: *Nika Sanftleben, Trude Eder, Ingeborg Halx*

Kostümentwürfe: *Liselotte Erler* • Anfertigung der Kostüme: *Louis Révy*
Technische Leitung: *Emil Hasler* • Einrichtung: *Hans Herrmann* • Beleuchtung: *Anton Hartmann*
Anfertigung der Dekorationen: *Friedrich Koburger* • Inspektion: *Anton Hackel* und *Edmund Meir*

Anfang **16 1/2** Uhr   Pause nach dem 2. Akt   Ende **19 1/2** Uhr

Die Walküre, excerpt (Leb wohl, du kühnes herrliches Kind!)

| Berlin | Staatskapelle | 78: Ultraphon F 205-206/FP 707-708 |
| 1929 | Meyrowitz | 78: Clangor MD 9143-9144/MD 9149-9150 |

| Berlin | BPO | 78: Telefunken E 1590 |
| 1933 | Borchard | LP: Telefunken GMA 57 |

HUGO WOLF (1860-1903)

Keine gleicht von allen Schönen

| Berlin | Raucheisen | Unpublished radio broadcast |
| 1942-1943 | | |

MISCELLANEOUS

Hans Reinmar can be seen and heard in the 1941 film **Der Weg ins Freie**, directed by Rolf Hansen and also starring Zarah Leander and Walther Ludwig

Turnus I

Donnerstag, den 14. Dezember 1933

Carmen

Oper in 4 Akten von Henry Meilhac und Ludovic Halévy

Musik von Georges Bizet

Inszenierung: Otto Krauß Musikalische Leitung: Wilhelm Franz Reuß

Gesamtausstattung: Gustav Bargo Spielleitung: Alexander d'Arnals

Kassenöffnung 18½ (6½) Uhr Anfang 19½ (7½) Uhr

Ende gegen 22¾ (10¾) Uhr

Don José, Sergeant in einem Dragonerregiment in Sevilla	Hans Fidesser
Zuniga, Leutnant } in demselben Regiment	Edwin Heyer
Moralès, Sergeant }	Rud. Ganszar
Carmen, eine Zigeunerin	Sigrid Onégin
Frasquita } Andalusische Arbeiterinnen	Margret Pfahl
Mercedes }	Charlotte Müller
Micaëla, navarresisches Bauernmädchen	Anita Gura
Escamillo, Stierkämpfer	Hans Reinmar
Dancairo, Anführer einer Schmugglerbande	Wilhelm Guttmann
Remendado, ein junger Schmuggler	Harry Steier
Lilas Pastia, Inhaber einer Vorstadtschenke	Fritz Kraft

Gerhard Hüsch
1901 -1984

Discography compiled
by John Hunt

FRANZ ABT (1819-1885)

Frühmorgens wenn die Hähne kräh'n

Berlin April 1937	Orchestra and Chorus Müller	78: Electrola EG 3952

JOHANN SEBASTIAN BACH (1685-1750)

Cantata No 56 "Ich will den Kreuzstab gerne tragen"

Tokyo July 1952	Victor Chamber Orchestra & Chorus Gurlitt	78: Victor (Japan) SD 3079-3080/JAS 251 LP: Victor (Japan) LS 2006

Schweig, aufgetürmtes Meer! (Cantata No 81)

Leipzig January 1933	Thomanerchor Gewandhaus Orchestra Straube	Untraced radio broadcast

Matthäus-Passion

Leipzig March 1941	Part of Christus Lemnitz, Beckmann, Erb, Schulze Thomanerchor Gewandhaus Orchestra Ramin	78: Electrola DB 7625-7640 78: HMV DB 6516-6531/DB 9165-9180 auto LP: Electrola E 83020-83022 LP: Eterna 820 625-820 627 LP: EMI 1C 147 29191-29193/EX 29 12203 LP: Calig CAL 30859-30860 CD: Calig 50859-50860 CD: Preiser 90228 <u>Excerpts</u> LP: Electrola E 91271

32 Hüsch

LUDWIG VAN BEETHOVEN (1770-1827)

Andenken (Ich denke dein)

Berlin December 1936	Müller	78: HMV DB 4497 78: Victor 12247 78: Victor (Japan) SD 36 LP: Preiser LV 105 LP: Arabesque 8136
Berlin February 1937	Müller	Electrola unpublished
Berlin June 1937	Müller	Electrola unpublished

An die ferne Geliebte, song cycle

Berlin December 1936	Müller	Electrola unpublished
Berlin February 1937	Müller	Electrola unpublished
Berlin June 1937	Müller	78: HMV DB 4496-4497 78: Victor 12246-12247 78: Victor (Japan) SD 35-36 LP: Arabesque 8136 LP: Preiser LV 105 CD: Preiser 89202

Die Ehre Gottes/Gellert-Lieder (Die Himmel rühmen des Ewigen Ehre)

Berlin October 1930	Staatskapelle Weissmann	78: Parlophone B 12345/R 972 78: Parlophone (Australia) A 3244 78: Odeon O-25810 78: Decca (USA) 20021 78: Columbia (Japan) J 5362/P 24/38782

GEORGES BIZET (1838-1875)

Les pêcheurs de perles, excerpt (Au fond du temple saint)

Berlin October 1934	Wittrisch Staatskapelle Müller <u>Sung in German</u>	78: Electrola DB 4430 LP: Electrola E 60563 LP: Top Classic TC 9044 LP: Historia H 8903 LP: Preiser LV 98 CD: Preiser 89024

JOHANNES BRAHMS (1833-1897)

Feldeinsamkeit (Ich ruhe still im hohen grünen Gras)

Berlin November 1934	Müller	Electrola unpublished
Berlin December 1934	Müller	78: Electrola EG 3308 LP: Rococo 5351 LP: Preiser LV 257 LP: EMI RLS 154 7003 LP: Arabesque 8136

Von ewiger Liebe (Dunkel, wie dunkel, in Wald und in Flur)

Berlin January 1936	Müller	Electrola unpublished

Wie bist du, meine Königin?

Berlin November 1934	Müller	78: Electrola EG 6779/EG 3308 LP: Rococo 5351 LP: Preiser LV 257 LP: EMI RLS 154 7003 LP: Arabesque 8136

Wir wandelten, wir zwei zusammen

Berlin January 1936	Müller	Electrola unpublished

GIACOMO CARISSIMI (1605-1674)

Vittoria, vittoria, mio core!

Berlin August 1936	Müller	Electrola unpublished

PETER CORNELIUS (1824-1874)

Christkind/Weihnachtslieder

Berlin October 1935	Orchestra and Chorus Müller	Electrola unpublished
Berlin November 1935	Orchestra and Chorus Müller	78: Electrola EH 944

Christus/Weihnachtslieder

Berlin October 1935	Orchestra and Chorus Müller	Electrola unpublished
Berlin November 1935	Orchestra and Chorus Müller	78: Electrola EH 944

Christus der Kinderfreund/Weihnachtslieder

Berlin October 1935	Orchestra and Chorus Müller	Electrola unpublished
Berlin November 1935	Orchestra and Chorus Müller	78: Electrola EH 944

Cornelius Lieder/concluded

Die 3 Könige/Weihnachtslieder

Berlin October 1935	Orchestra and Chorus Müller	78: Electrola unpublished
Berlin November 1935	Orchestra and Chorus Müller	78: Electrola EH 944

Die Hirten/Weihnachtslieder

Berlin October 1935	Orchestra and Chorus Müller	Electrola unpublished
Berlin November 1935	Orchestra and Chorus Müller	78: Electrola EH 944

Komm', wir wandeln zusammen

Berlin August 1936	Müller	Electrola unpublished

Simeon/Weihnachtslieder

Berlin October 1935	Orchestra and Chorus Müller	Electrola unpublished
Berlin November 1935	Orchestra and Chorus Müller	78: Electrola EH 944

36   Hüsch

EUGEN D'ALBERT (1864-1932)

Meine Liebe, mein Glück

Berlin	Bäumer	78: Parlophone B 48192
April 1932	Staatskapelle	78: Odeon O-25096
	Weissmann	LP: Preiser LV 76
		LP: Rococo 5248

Tiefland, excerpt (Nun hab' ich nichts als dich mehr!)

Berlin	Bäumer	78: Parlophone B 48192
April 1932	Staatskapelle	78: Odeon O-25096
	Weissmann	LP: Preiser LV 76

EMMEL

Du Vaterland

Berlin	Salon-orchester	78: Electrola EG 2635
October	Schönbaumsfeld	
1932		

HANS GANSSER

Deutschland erwache!

| Berlin | Berlin SO | 78: Telefunken E 1381 |
| 1932 | F.A.Schmidt | |

UMBERTO GIORDANO (1867-1948)

Andrea Chenier, excerpt (Nemico della patria)

Berlin	Staatskapelle	78: Electrola DB 4510
October	Müller	LP: Rococo 5248
1937	Sung in German	CD: Preiser 89071

CHARLES GOUNOD (1818-1893)

Faust, excerpt (Avant de quitter ces lieux)

Berlin	Staatskapelle	78: Electrola EG 6136/JK 2607
September	Müller	LP: Preiser LV 285
1937	Sung in German	CD: Preiser 89071

PAUL GRAENER (1872-1944)

Der Page sprach

Berlin	Müller	78: Electrola EG 3544
November		LP: Preiser LV 208
1935		

Der Palmstrom

Berlin	Müller	78: Electrola EG 3544
November		LP: Electrola E 83393
1935		LP: Preiser LV 208
		LP: Toshiba EAC 77365-77368

Philantropisch

Berlin	Müller	78: Electrola EG 3544
November		LP: Electrola E 83393
1935		LP: Preiser LV 208
		LP: Toshiba EAC 77365-77368

38 Hüsch

GEORGE FRIDERIC HANDEL (1685-1759)

Giulio Cesare, excerpt (V'adoro pupille)

Berlin	Staatskapelle	78: Electrola EH 925/12090
May 1935	Müller	78: Victor (Japan) JD 1583/ND 766
	<u>Sung in German</u>	LP: Rococo 5351
		LP: Preiser LV 76

HELMUND

Deutschland, blühe neu auf!

Berlin	Orchestra	78: Odeon O-11740
November	and Chorus	
1932	Dobrindt	

HUGO HERMANN

Der Dichter spricht, arranged by Dobrindt

Berlin	Orchestra	78: Parlophone B 48206/R 1781
May 1932	Dobrindt	78: Parlophone (Australia) A 3892
		78: Odeon O-25811

Ich bin geboren, deutsch zu fühlen

Berlin	Orchestra	78: Parlophone B 48275
August	and Chorus	78: Odeon O-25026
1932	Dobrindt	

Ein jedes Volk bestimmt sich seinen Herrn

Berlin	Orchestra	78: Parlophone B 48275
August	and Chorus	78: Odeon O-25026
1932	Dobrindt	

Mahnung

Berlin	Orchestra	78: Parlophone B 48275
August	and Chorus	78: Odeon O-25026
1932	Dobrindt	

Salomo, arranged by Dobrindt

Berlin	Orchestra	78: Parlophone B 48206/R 1781
May 1932	Dobrindt	78: Parlophone (Australia) A 3892
		78: Odeon O-25811
		LP: Preiser LV 76

Wir wollen sein ein einig Volk von Brüdern

Berlin	Orchestra	78: Parlophone B 48275
August	and Chorus	78: Odeon O-25026
1932	Dobrindt	

EUGEN HILDACH (1849-1924)

Wo du hingehst

Berlin August 1934	Orchestra Müller	78: Electrola EG 3153/EG 3299/EG 6779

FERDINAND HILLER (1811-1885)

Gebet (Herr, den ich tief im Herzen trage)

Berlin August 1934	Orchestra Müller	78: Electrola EG 3153

HOESER

Frühling am Rhein

Berlin June 1929	Raucheisen	Parlophone/Odeon unpublished
Berlin October 1932	Salon-orchester Schönbaumsfeld	78: Electrola EG 2635

ENGELBERT HUMPERDINCK (1854-1921)

Am Rhein

Berlin June 1929	Raucheisen	Parlophone/Odeon unpublished

Hänsel und Gretel, excerpt (Besenbinderlied)

Berlin   Chorus member   78: Electrola EH 1024
January   Staatskapelle   78: Victor (Japan) JD 1704/ND 699
1937   Müller   LP: Electrola E 83393
                                  LP: Preiser LV 76
                                  LP: EMI EX 29 01693
                                  LP: Toshiba EAC 77365-77368
                                  LP: Arabesque 8022
                                  CD: Nimbus NI 7848
                                  CD: Preiser 89071

Königskinder, excerpt (Verdorben! Gestorben!)

Berlin   Staatskapelle   78: Electrola EH 1024
January   and Chorus   78: Victor JD 1704/ND 699
1937   Müller   LP: Preiser LV 76
                                  LP: Arabesque 8022
                                  CD: Preiser 89071
                                  <u>LV 76 incorrectly dated 1926</u>

YRYO KILPINEN (1892-1959)

Abendsonnenstrahlen

Tokyo 1962	Kobayashi	LP: Victor (Japan) RA 2189 <u>Televised performance</u>

Alte Kirche/Fjeldlieder

Berlin January 1936	Staatskapelle Müller	78: HMV DA 1495 LP: Preiser LV 80 CD: Preiser 89103

Am Kirchenstrande/Fjeldlieder

Berlin January 1936	Staatskapelle Müller	78: HMV DA 1495 LP: Preiser LV 80 CD: Preiser 89103

An das Lied/Fjeldlieder

Berlin January 1936	Staatskapelle Müller	78: HMV DA 1496 LP: Preiser LV 80 CD: Preiser 89103

Anmutiger Vertrag/Lieder der Liebe

London February 1935	M.Kilpinen	HMV unpublished
Berlin March 1935	M.Kilpinen	78: HMV DB 2597 LP: Preiser LV 80 CD: Preiser 89103

Auf einem verfallenen Kirchhof/Lieder um den Tod

London February 1935	M.Kilpinen	78: HMV DB 2595 CD: Preiser 89103

Kilpinen songs/continued

Deine Rosen an der Brust

London M.Kilpinen HMV unpublished
February
1935

Elegie an die Nachtigall

Berlin M.Kilpinen 78: HMV DB 2594
March 1935 LP: Preiser LV 80
  CD: Preiser 89103

Tokyo Kobayashi LP: Victor (Japan) RA 2189
1962 <u>Televised performance</u>

Es zittert meine Seele

Tokyo Kobayashi LP: Victor (Japan) RA 2189
1962 <u>Televised performance</u>

Den Fjelden zu /Fjeldlieder

Berlin M.Kilpinen 78: HMV DA 1495
January LP: Preiser LV 80
1936 CD: Preiser 89103

Fjeldlied/Fjeldlieder

Berlin M.Kilpinen 78: HMV DA 1496
January LP: Preiser LV 80
1936 CD: Preiser 89103

Die Fusswaschung

London M.Kilpinen HMV unpublished
February
1935

44 Hüsch

Kilpinen songs/continued

Heimat/Lieder der Liebe

London February 1935	M.Kilpinen	HMV unpublished
Berlin March 1935	M.Kilpinen	78: HMV DB 2596 LP: Preiser LV 80 CD: Preiser 89103

Ich liebe deinen Frieden

Tokyo 1962	Kobayashi	LP: Victor (Japan) RA 2189 <u>Televised performance</u>

Ich sang mich durch das deutsche Land /Spielmannslieder

London February 1935	M.Kilpinen	HMV unpublished
Berlin March 1935	M.Kilpinen	78: HMV DB 2597 LP: Preiser LV 80 CD: Preiser 89103

Im Mondschein

Tokyo 1962	Kobayashi	LP: Victor (Japan) RA 2189 <u>Televised performance</u>

In der Felder trauervollem Wogen

Tokyo 1962	Kobayashi	LP: Victor (Japan) RA 2189 <u>Televised performance</u>

In der Sommernacht

Tokyo 1962	Kobayashi	LP: Victor (Japan) RA 2189 <u>Televised performance</u>

Kilpinen songs/continued

Jugendflucht

Tokyo 1962	Kobayashi	LP: Victor (Japan) RA 2189 <u>Televised performance</u>

Kleines Lied/Lieder der Liebe

London February 1935	M.Kilpinen	HMV unpublished
Berlin March 1935	M.Kilpinen	78: HMV DB 2596 LP: Preiser LV 80 CD: Preiser 89103

Marienkirche zu Danzig im Gerüst

Berlin March 1935	M.Kilpinen	78: HMV DB 2598 LP: Preiser LV 80 CD: Preiser 89103

Mondschein

London February 1935	M.Kilpinen	78: HMV DB 2594 LP: Preiser LV 80 CD: Preiser 89103

Das Moor/Fjeldlieder

Berlin January 1936	Staatskapelle Müller	78: HMV DA 1495 LP: Preiser LV 80 CD: Preiser 89103

Nacht hüllt den Hof

Tokyo 1962	Kobayashi	LP: Victor (Japan) RA 2189 <u>Televised performance</u>

Kilpinen songs/continued

Nachtviolen

Tokyo 1962	Kobayashi	LP: Victor (Japan) RA 2189 <u>Televised performance</u>

Der Säemann /Lieder um den Tod

London February 1935	M.Kilpinen	HMV unpublished
Berlin March 1935	M.Kilpinen	78: HMV DB 2596 LP: Preiser LV 80 CD: Preiser 89103

Der Skiläufer

Berlin March 1935	M.Kilpinen	78: HMV DB 2594 LP: Preiser LV 80 CD: Preiser 89103

Spielmannssehnen/Spielmannslieder

London February 1935	M.Kilpinen	HMV unpublished
Berlin March 1935	M.Kilpinen	78: HMV DB 2597 CD: Preiser 89103

Tanzlied /Spielmannslieder

London February 1935	M.Kilpinen	HMV unpublished
Berlin March 1935	M.Kilpinen	78: HMV DB 2597 LP: Preiser LV 80 CD: Preiser 89103

Der Tod und der einsame Trinker/Lieder um den Tod

London February 1935	M.Kilpinen	78: HMV DB 2595 CD: Preiser 89103

Kilpinen songs/continued

Ueber die tausend Berge/Lieder der Liebe

London February 1935	M.Kilpinen	HMV unpublished
Berlin March 1935	M.Kilpinen	78: HMV DB 2596 LP: Preiser LV 80 CD: Preiser 89103

Unverlierbare Gewähr/Lieder um den Tod

London February 1935	M.Kilpinen	HMV unpublished
Berlin March 1935	M.Kilpinen	78: HMV DB 2596 LP: Preiser LV 80 CD: Preiser 89103

Venezianisches Intermezzo

Berlin March 1935	M.Kilpinen	78: HMV DB 2598 LP: Electrola E 83393 LP: Preiser LV 80 LP: Toshiba EAC 77365-77368 CD: Preiser 89103

Vergänglichkeit

Tokyo 1962	Kobayashi	LP: Victor (Japan) RA 2189 <u>Televised performance</u>

Vergissmeinnicht

Berlin March 1935	M.Kilpinen	78: HMV DB 2597 LP: Preiser LV 80 CD: Preiser 89103

Vöglein Schwermut/Lieder um den Tod

London February 1935	M.Kilpinen	78: HMV DB 2595 LP: Preiser LV 80 CD: Preiser 89103

Kilpinen songs/concluded

Von zwei Rosen

London February 1935	M.Kilpinen	HMV unpublished

Winternacht/Lieder um den Tod

London February 1935	M.Kilpinen	78: HMV DB 2595 CD: Preiser 89103

Wunder

Tokyo 1962	Kobayashi	LP: Victor (Japan) RA 2189 <u>Televised performance</u>

CONRADIN KREUTZER (1780-1849)

Das ist der Tag des Herrn

Berlin February 1937	Orchestra and Chorus Müller	78: Electrola EG 3952

Das Nachtlager von Granada, excerpt (Trenne nicht das Band der Liebe)

Berlin February 1934	E.Friedrich, W.Ludwig Staatskapelle Zaun	Electrola unpublished
Berlin March 1934	E.Friedrich, W.Ludwig Staatskapelle Zaun	78: Electrola EH 864/FKX 174 LP: Preiser LV 76 <u>LV 76 incorrectly dated 1933</u>

Das Nachtlager von Granada, excerpt (Schon die Abendglocken klangen)

Berlin February 1934	E.Friedrich, W.Ludwig, Strienz Staatskapelle Zaun	Electrola unpublished
Berlin March 1934	E.Friedrich W.Ludwig, Strienz Staatskapelle Zaun	78: Electrola EH 864/FKX 174 LP: Preiser LV 120

CARL LOEWE (1796–1869)

Archibald Douglas (Ich hab' es getragen sieben Jahr')

Berlin June 1929	Raucheisen	78: Parlophone E 11362 78: Odeon O-6924 78: Decca (USA) 25755 78: Columbia (Japan) JW 123 LP: Preiser LV 200/LV 257
Berlin April 1939	Muller	78: Electrola DB 4669 78: HMV (Australia) ED 200

Fridericus rex, unser König und Herr

Berlin December 1928	Staatskapelle Weissmann	Parlophone/Odeon unpublished
Berlin June 1929	Raucheisen	78: Parlophone P 9447/B 48281 78: Odeon O-25077 78: Odeon (Austria) 169180

Heinrich der Vogler (Herr Heinrich sitzt am Vogelherd)

Berlin December 1928	Weissmann	78: Parlophone R 2496 78: Odeon O-25932
Berlin November 1934	Städtische Oper Orchestra Müller	78: Electrola EG 3207/JE 71

Loewe ballads/concluded

Prinz Eugen (Zelte, Posten, Wer-da-Rufer)

Berlin December 1928	Staatskapelle Weissmann	Parlophone/Odeon unpublished
Berlin June 1929	Raucheisen	78: Parlophone P 9447/B 4828/R 2496 78: Odeon O-25077 78: Odeon (Austria) 169180 CD: Pearl GEMMCD 9251
Berlin November 1934	Städtische Oper Orchestra Müller	78: Electrola EG 3207/JE 71

Süsses Begräbnis (Schäferin, ach wie haben sie dich so süss begraben!)

Berlin June 1929	Raucheisen	78: Parlophone P 65676/E 11336 78: Parlophone (Australia) A 4496

Tom der Reimer (Der Reimer Thomas lag am Bach)

Berlin June 1929	Raucheisen	78: Parlophone P 9519/E 11336/P 67576 78: Parlophone (Australia) A 4496

Die Uhr (Ich trage, wo ich gehe)

Berlin December 1928	Staatskapelle Weissmann	78: Parlophone P 9516 78: Odeon O-6879

ALBERT LORTZING (1801-1851)

Undine

Stuttgart March 1938	Role of Kühleborn Eipperle, Buchta, Ostertag Reichssender Orchestra & Chorus Zimmermann	Unpublished radio broadcast

Undine, excerpt (Nun ist's vollbracht/O kehr zurück!)

Berlin June 1932	Bettendorf Orchestra and Chorus Weissmann	78: Parlophone B 48219 78: Odeon O-25095
Berlin September 1935	Chorus member Orchestra and Chorus Müller	78: Electrola EH 936/FKX 132 78: Victor (Japan) JB 128 LP: Rococo 5248 LP: Preiser LV 285 CD: Preiser 89071

Undine, excerpt (An des Rheines grünen Ufern)

Berlin September 1935	Orchestra and Chorus Müller	78: Electrola EH 936/FKX 132 LP: Preiser LV 76 CD: Preiser 89071

Der Wildschütz, excerpt (Wie freundlich strahlt/Heiterkeit und Fröhlichkeit)

Berlin October 1928	Staatskapelle Weissmann	78: Odeon O-7705/O-7833 LP: Preiser 5248 LP: Preiser LV 285 CD: Nimbus NI 7867

Zar und Zimmermann, excerpt (Auf, Gesellen!)

Berlin September 1937	Staatskapelle and Chorus Müller	78: Electrola EH 1069 LP: Arabesque 8022

Zar und Zimmermann, excerpt (Sonst spielt' ich mit Zepter)

Berlin October 1928	Staatskapelle Weissmann	78: Parlophone E 11091 78: Parlophone (Australia) A 4323 78: Odeon O-7833 LP: Rococo 5248 LP: Preiser LV 285 LP: BBC Records REH 716 CD: BBC Records CD 716 REH 716 incorrectly dated 1929
Berlin September 1937	Staatskapelle Müller	78: Electrola EH 1069/FKX 132 LP: Arabesque 8022 CD: Preiser 89071

Meisterporträt Albert Lortzing
Unspecified extracts from Der Waffenschmied, Der Wildschütz and Zar und Zimmermann

Berlin January 1935	Frind, W.Ludwig, Strienz Orchestra and Chorus Müller	78: Electrola EH 907/FKX 182

PIETRO MASCAGNI (1863-1945)

Cavalleria rusticana, Querschnitt

Berlin 1932	A.Konetzni, Frind, Stellakis Berlin SO F.A.Schmidt Sung in German	78: Telefunken E 1296 78: Telefunken (Japan) 23680

WOLFGANG AMADEUS MOZART (1756-1791)

Così fan tutte, excerpt (Donne mie la fate a tanti)

Berlin April 1939	Staatskapelle Müller Sung in German	78: Electrola DA 4463 LP: Preiser LV 285 LP: EMI EX 29 05983 CD: EMI CMS 763 7052/CDM 763 7532 CD: Preiser 89071

Don Giovanni, excerpt (Finch' han dal vino!)

Berlin October 1928	Staatskapelle Weissmann Sung in German	78: Parlophone B 47050/R 2339 78: Odeon O-26150 78: Decca (USA) 20248 78: Record Rarities (USA) A 6743
Berlin April 1939	Staatskapelle Müller Sung in German	78: Electrola DA 4463

Don Giovanni, excerpt (Deh vieni alla finestra)

Berlin October 1928	Staatskapelle Weissmann Sung in German	78: Parlophone B 47050/R 2339 78: Odeon O-26150 78: Decca (USA) 20248 78: Record Rarities (USA) A 6743

Don Giovanni, excerpt (Madamina)

Berlin November 1931	Staatskapelle Weissmann Sung in German	78: Parlophone B 48106/R 1165 78: Parlophone (Australia) A 3414 78: Odeon O-25096 78: Decca (USA) 20022 78: Columbia (Japan) J 5551 LP: Rococo 5248

Don Giovanni, excerpt (Là ci darem la mano)

Berlin June 1932	Bettendorf Orchestra Weissmann <u>Sung in German</u>	78: Parlophone B 48261/R 1320 78: Parlophone (Australia) A 3553 78: Odeon O-25094 78: Decca (USA) 20010
Berlin February 1935	Perras Staatskapelle Müller <u>Sung in German</u>	78: Electrola DA 4374/DA 4408 78: Victor (Japan) NF 4170 LP: Rococo 5351 LP: Preiser LV 1312 LP: Arabeesque 8022

Le nozze di Figaro, excerpt (Se vuol ballare)

Berlin November 1931	Staatskapelle Weissmann <u>Sung in German</u>	78: Parlophone B 48094/R 1122 78: Parlophone (Australia) A 3356 78: Odeon O-25092 78: Decca (USA) 20009 78: Columbia (Japan) J 5402 LP: Rococo 5248

Le nozze di Figaro, excerpt (Non più andrai)

Berlin November 1931	Staatskapelle Weissmann <u>Sung in German</u>	78: Parlophone B 48094/R 1122 78: Parlophone (Australia) A 3356 78: Odeon O-25092 78: Decca (USA) 20009 LP: Rococo 5248
Berlin April 1939	Staatskapelle Müller <u>Sung in German</u>	78: Electrola DB 4681 LP: Arabesque 8022

Le nozze di Figaro, excerpt (Hai già vinta la causa!)

Berlin April 1939	Staatskapelle Müller <u>Sung in German</u>	78: Electrola DB 4681 LP: Electrola E 83393 LP: Preiser LV 285 LP: Toshiba EAC 77365-77368 LP: Arabesque 8022 CD: Preiser 89071

Die Zauberflöte

Berlin November 1937- March 1938	<u>Role of Papageno</u> Lemnitz, Berger, Beilke, Rosvaenge, Strienz, Grossmann Favres Solisten- vereinigung BPO Beecham	78: HMV DB 3465-3483/DB 8475-8493 auto 78: Electrola C 6371-6389 78: Victor M 541-542 78: Victor (Japan) JD 1467-1485 45: Victor WCT 56/WCT 6101 LP: HMV ALP 1273-1275 LP: Electrola E 80471-80473 LP: Victor LCT 6101 LP: World Records SH 158-160 LP: Toshiba GR 2115 LP: Vox (USA) MSE 1 LP: Turnabout TV 4113-4115/ THS 65078-65080 LP: Calig CAL 30845-30846 LP: Angel 6129 LP: EMI RLS 143 4653 CD: EMI CHS 761 0342 CD: Nimbus NI 7827-7828 CD: Pearl GEMMCDS 9371 CD: Calig 30845-30846 CD: Melodram MEL 27056 CD: Dutton 2CDEA 5011 <u>Excerpts</u> 78: Electrola DB 4682 LP: Electrola E 83393 LP: HMV ALP 1870 LP: World Records SHB 47/SHB 100 LP: EMI 1C 147 28989-28990 LP: Toshiba EAC 77365-77368 CD: Nimbus NI 7822 CD: Memoir CDMOIR 406 <u>March 1938 sessions conducted by Seidler-Winkler</u>

Die Zauberflöte, excerpt (Der Vogelfänger bin ich ja)

Berlin April 1930	Staatskapelle Weissmann	78: Parlophone B 12455/R 979 78: Parlophone (Australia) A 3286 78: Odeon O-25093 78: Decca (USA) 20036 78: Columbia (Japan) J 5402 LP: Preiser LV 76

Die Zauberflöte, excerpt (Bei Männern, welche Liebe fühlen)

Berlin January 1931	Schöne Berlin RO Walter	Untraced radio broadcast
Berlin June 1932	Bettendorf Orchestra Weissmann	78: Parlophone B 48261/R 1320 78: Parlophone (Australia) A 3553 78: Odeon O-25094 78: Decca (USA) 20010
Berlin February 1935	Perras Staatskapelle Müller	78: Electrola DA 4374/DA 4408 78: Victor (Japan) NF 4170 LP: Rococo 5351 LP: Preiser LV 1312 LP: EMI EX 29 05983 LP: Arabesque 8022

Die Zauberflöte, excerpt (Ein Mädchen oder Weibchen)

Berlin April 1930	Staatskapelle Weissmann	78: Parlophone E 11046 78: Parlophone (Australia) A 4280 78: Odeon O-7705 78: Decca (USA) 25443 LP: Preiser LV 76
Berlin January 1931	Berlin RO Walter	Untraced radio broadcast

Oiseaux si tous les ans

Berlin August 1936	Müller Sung in German	Electrola unpublished

Sehsucht nach dem Frühlinge (Komm', lieber Mai!)

Berlin August 1936	Müller	Electrola unpublished

Hüsch

OTTO NICOLAI (1810-1849)

Die lustigen Weiber von Windsor, excerpt (Gott grüss' euch, Sir!/In einem Waschkorb?)

Berlin	E.Fuchs	78: Columbia (Germany) DW 3047
January	Städtische Oper	LP: Preiser LV 76
1933	Orchestra	CD: Preiser 89071
	Zemlinsky	<u>LV 76 incorrectly dated 1934</u>

SIEGFRIED OCHS (1858-1925)

Dank sei dir Herr!, previously attributed to Handel

Berlin	Staatskapelle	78: Electrola EH 925/12090
May 1935	Müller	78: Victor (Japan) JD 1583/ND 766
		LP: Electrola E 83393
		LP: Toshiba EAC 77365-77368

HANS PFITZNER (1869-1949)

Der arme Heinrich, excerpt (Du bist wie Kinder eben sind)

Berlin May 1934	Knepel Berlin RO	Unpublished radio broadcast

Abbitte

Berlin December 1939	Pfitzner	78: Electrola DA 4477 LP: Electrola E 60051 LP: Toshiba HB 1034/AA 9545 LP: Preiser LV 208 CD: EMI CDC 555 2252 CD: Preiser 90029

Es fällt ein Stern herunter

Berlin March 1934	Orchestra Müller	78: Electrola EG 3018 LP: Preiser LV 76

Die Einsame

Berlin December 1939	Pfitzner	78: Electrola DA 4476 LP: Electrola E 60051 LP: Toshiba HB 1034/AA 9545 LP: Preiser LV 208 CD: Preiser 90029

Der Gärtner (Wohin ich geh' und schaue)

Berlin December 1939	Pfitzner	78: Electrola DA 4476 LP: Electrola E 60051 LP: Toshiba HB 1034/AA 9545 LP: Preiser LV 208 CD: Preiser 90029

Pfitzner Lieder/continued

Hast du von den Fischerkindern

Berlin February 1938	Pfitzner	78: Electrola DA 4439/DA 4475 78: Victor (Japan) JA 434/NF 4171 LP: Electrola E 60051 LP: Toshiba HB 1034/AA 9545 LP: Preiser LV 208 CD: EMI CDC 555 2252

Herbstgefühl

Berlin February 1938	Pfitzner	78: Electrola DA 4439 78: Victor (Japan) JA 434/NF 4171 LP: Preiser LV 208 CD: Preiser 90029 CD: EMI CDC 555 2252

Hussens Kerker (Es geht mit mir zu Ende)

Berlin February 1938	Pfitzner	LP: Preiser LV 208 CD: Preiser 90029 CD: EMI CDC 555 2252

In Danzig (Dunkle Giebel, hohe Fenster)

Berlin December 1939	Pfitzner	78: Electrola DA 4477 LP: Electrola E 60051 LP: Preiser LV 208 CD: Preiser 90029 CD: EMI CDC 555 2252

Ist der Himmel darum im Lenz so blau?

Berlin March 1934	Orchestra Müller	Electrola unpublished
Berlin August 1936	Müller	CD: Preiser 90029

Pfitzner Lieder/continued

Klage

Berlin March 1934	Orchestra Müller	78: Electrola EG 3018 LP: Preiser LV 76

Leuchtende Tage

Berlin August 1936	Müller	Electrola unpublished
Berlin February 1938	Pfitzner	78: Electrola DA 4439 78: Victor (Japan) JA 434/NF 4171 LP: Preiser LV 208 CD: Preiser 90029 CD: EMI CDC 555 2252

Michaelskirchplatz

Berlin February 1938	Pfitzner	LP: Preiser LV 208
Berlin December 1939	Pfitzner	78: Electrola DA 4478 LP: Electrola E 60051 LP: Toshiba HB 1034/AA 9545 CD: Preiser 90029

Nachts (Ich stehe in Waldesschatten)

Berlin December 1939	Pfitzner	78: Electrola DA 4478 LP: Electrola E 60051 LP: Preiser LV 208 LP: Toshiba HB 1034/AA 9545 CD: Preiser 90029 CD: EMI CDC 555 2252

Pfitzner Lieder/concluded

Säerspruch

Berlin February 1938	Pfitzner	LP: Preiser LV 208 CD: Preiser 90029 CD: EMI CDC 555 2252

Zum Abschied meiner Tochter (Der Herbstwind schüttelt die Linde)

Berlin December 1939	Pfitzner	78: Electrola DA 4475 LP: Electrola E 60051 LP: Toshiba HB 1034/AA 9545 LP: Preiser LV 208 CD: Preiser 90029

ROBERT PLANQUETTE (1848-1903)

Surcouf

Berlin June 1931	Role of Surcouf Berlin RO Orthmann Sung in German	Untraced radio broadcast

GUSTAV ADOLF PRESSEL (1827-1890)

An der Weser

Berlin October 1930	Staatskapelle Weissmann	78: Parlophone B 12345 78: Odeon O-25810

GIACOMO PUCCINI (1858-1924)

La Bohème, excerpt (Ah Mimì tu più non torni!)

Berlin October 1937	Rosvaenge Staatskapelle Seidler-Winkler Sung in German	78: Electrola DB 4499 LP: Rococo 5375 LP: Eterna (USA) 721 CD: Pearl GEMMCD 9394 CD: Preiser 89211

Madama Butterfly, excerpts (Dovunque al mondo; Addio fiorito asil)

Berlin February 1934	W.Ludwig Staatskapelle Zaun Sung in German	78: Electrola EG 3035 78: Victor (Japan) JE 119 CD: Preiser 89088

Tosca, excerpts (Tre sbirri, una carozza!; La povera mia cena)

Berlin June 1937	Orchestra and Chorus Müller	CD: Preiser 89071
Berlin June 1937	Orchestra and Chorus Müller Sung in German	78: Electrola DB 4485 LP: Rococo 5248 LP: Preiser LV 285

64   Hüsch

RASCH

Ich hab' mich ganz verloren

Berlin   Müller   78: Electrola EG 6343
March 1938   LP: Rococo 5351
                                 LP: Preiser LV 208

Wenn ich dereinst

Berlin   Müller   78: Electrola EG 6343
March 1938

EMIL VON REZNICEK (1860-1945)

Das Regiment Forkade bei Hochkirch

Berlin   Orchestra   78: Odeon O-11740
November   and Chorus
1932   Dobrindt

FRANZ SCHUBERT (1797-1828)

Abschied/Schwanengesang (Ade, du muntre, du fröhliche Stadt!)

Berlin August 1937	Moore	LP: World Records SHB 65 LP: Toshiba EAC 77365-77368 LP: Arabesque 8107 CD: Toshiba Shinseido SRG 1004 CD: Preiser 89017
Tokyo July 1952	Gurlitt	78: Victor (Japan) SF 716/JAS 249 LP: Victor (Japan) LS 103-104
Tokyo 1952	Gurlitt	LP: King (Japan) K200 488 CD: King (Japan) K32Y 190
Tokyo 1962	Mitsuishi	LP: Victor (Japan) RA 2189 <u>Televised performance</u>

Am Feierabend/Die schöne Müllerin (Hätt' ich tausend Arme zu rühren)

London January 1935	Müller	78: HMV DB 2430/DB 7829 78: Victor (Japan) JD 725/ND 204 LP: Victor (Japan) LT 110 LP: Electrola E 80685 LP: Angel DTX 20036 LP: Preiser LV 204 LP: World Records SH 295 LP: Melodiya D030911-030912 LP: Toshiba GR 2156/EAC 77365-77368 LP: Arabesque 8107 CD: Pearl GEMMCD 9479 CD: Toshiba Shinseido SRG 1004 CD: Preiser 89202

Am Meer/Schwanengesang (Das Meer erglänzte weit hinaus)

Berlin August 1937	Moore	LP: World Records SHB 65 LP: Toshiba EAC 77365-77368 LP: Arabesque 8107 CD: Toshiba Shinseido SRG 1004 CD: Preiser 89017
Tokyo July 1952	Gurlitt	78: Victor (Japan) SD 3074/JAS 249 LP: Victor (Japan) LS 103-104

Schubert Lieder/continued

An die Leier (Ich will von Atreus Söhnen)

Berlin November 1942	Müller	Unpublished radio broadcast

An die Musik (Du holde Kunst, in wieviel grauen Stunden)

Berlin   Müller   78: HMV DA 4445
May 1938   LP: Rococo 5351
                            LP: World Records SHB 65
                            LP: Preiser LV 257
                            LP: Arabesque 8107
                            CD: Toshiba Shinseido SRG 1004
                            CD: Preiser 89017

Tokyo   Gurlitt   78: Victor (Japan) SF 719/JAS 275
July 1952   45: Victor (Japan) ES 8031
                            LP: Victor (Japan) LS 2006

An die Türen will ich schleichen/Gesänge des Harfners

Berlin   Müller   78: Electrola DA 4466
January   LP: Preiser LV 105
1939   LP: Arabesque 8136
                            CD: Toshiba Shinseido SRG 1004
                            CD: Preiser 89017

Der Atlas/Schwanengesang (Ich unglücksel'ger Atlas!)

Tokyo   Gurlitt   78: Victor (Japan) SF 717/JAS 249
July 1952   LP: Victor (Japan) LS 103-104

Tokyo   Gurlitt   LP: King (Japan) K200 488
1952   CD: King (Japan) K32Y 190

Schubert Lieder/continued

Auf dem Fluss/Winterreise (Der du so lustig rauschtest)

London April 1933	Müller	HMV unpublished
Berlin August 1933	Müller	78: HMV DA 1344 78: Victor (Japan) JI 50/NFB 1 LP: Victor JF 1-2/LH 16 LP: Electrola E 80679-80680 LP: Preiser LV 203 LP: World Records SHB 65 LP: Toshiba HD 1032-1033/GR 2139-2140/ EAC 77365-77368 LP: EMI 1C 137 53032-53036M LP: Arabesque 8107 CD: Pearl GEMMCD 9469 CD: Toshiba Shinseido SRG 1004 CD: Preiser 89202

Aufenthalt/Schwanengesang (Rauschender Strom, brausender Wald!)

Tokyo July 1952	Gurlitt	78: Victor (Japan) SF 716/JAS 249 LP: Victor (Japan) LS 103-104

Des Baches Wiegenlied/Die schöne Müllerin (Gute Ruh'! Gute Ruh'!)

London February 1935	Müller	78: HMV DB 2436/DB 7828 78: Victor (Japan) JD 731/ND 198 LP: Victor (Japan) LT 110 LP: Electrola E 80685 LP: Angel DTX 20036 LP: Preiser LV 204 LP: World Records SH 295 LP: Melodiya D030911-030912 LP: Toshiba GR 2156/EAC 77365-77368 LP: Arabesque 8107 CD: Pearl GEMMCD 9479 CD: Toshiba Shinseido SRG 1004 CD: Preiser 89202

Der blinde Knabe (O sag', ihr Lieben, mir einmal)

Tokyo 1962	Mitsuishi	LP: Victor (Japan) RA 2189 Televised performance

Schubert Lieder/continued

Die böse Farbe/Die schöne Müllerin (Ich möchte zieh'n in die Welt hinaus)

London February 1935	Müller	78: HMV DB 2435/DB 7829 78: Victor (Japan) JD 730/ND 199 LP: Victor (Japan) LT 110 LP: Electrola E 80685 LP: Angel DTX 20036 LP: Preiser LV 204 LP: World Records SH 295 LP: Melodiya D030911-030912 LP: Toshiba GR 2156/EAC 77365-77368 LP: Arabesque 8107 CD: Pearl GEMMCD 9479 CD: Toshiba Shinseido SRG 1004 CD: Preiser 89202

Danksagung an den Bach/Die schöne Müllerin (War es also gemeint?)

London January 1935	Müller	78: HMV DB 2429/DB 7828 78: Victor (Japan) JD 724/ND 198 45: Victor (Japan) EK 13 LP: Victor (Japan) LT 110 LP: Electrola E 80685 LP: Angel DTX 20036 LP: Preiser LV 204 LP: World Records SH 295 LP: Melodiya D030911-030912 LP: Toshiba GR 2156/EAC 77365-77368 LP: Arabesque 8107 CD: Pearl GEMMCD 9479 CD: Toshiba Shinseido SRG 1004 CD: Preiser 89202

Dass sie hier gewesen (Dass der Ostwind Düfte hauchet in die Lüfte)

Berlin January 1939	Müller	78: Electrola DA 4466 LP: Preiser LV 257 LP: Arabesque 8136 CD: Preiser 89017

Schubert Lieder/continued

Der Doppelgänger/Schwanengesang (Still ist die Nacht, es ruhen die Gassen)

Berlin August 1937	Moore	HMV unpublished
Berlin April 1939	Müller	78: Electrola DB 5523 78: Victor (Japan) ND 172/RL 66 LP: World Records SHB 65 LP: Preiser LV 257 LP: Toshiba EAC 77365-77368 LP: Arabesque 8107 CD: Toshiba Shinseido SRG 1004 CD: Preiser 89017
Tokyo July 1952	Gurlitt	78: Victor (Japan) SD 3075/JAS 249 45: Victor (Japan) ES 8013 LP: Victor (Japan) LS 103-104
Tokyo 1952	Gurlitt	LP: King (Japan) K20C 488 CD: King (Japan) K32Y 190

Eifersucht und Stolz/Die schöne Müllerin(Wohin so schnell, so kraus und wild?)

London February 1935	Müller	78: HMV DB 2434/DB 7830 78: Victor (Japan) JD 729/ND 200 LP: Victor (Japan) LT 110 LP: Electrola E 80685 LP: Angel DTX 20036 LP: Preiser LV 204 LP: World Records SH 295 LP: Melodiya D030911-030912 LP: Toshiba GR 2156/EAC 77365-77368 LP: Arabesque 8107 CD: Pearl GEMMCD 9479 CD: Toshiba Shinseido SRG 1004 CD: Preiser 89202

Schubert Lieder/continued

Einsamkeit/Winterreise (Wie eine trübe Wolke)

London April 1933	Müller	78: HMV DA 1345 78: Victor (Japan) JI 51/NFB 2 LP: Victor JF 1-2/LH 16 LP: Electrola E 80679-80680 LP: Preiser LV 203 LP: World Records SHB 65 LP: Toshiba HD 1032-1033/GR 2139-2140/ EAC 77365-77368 LP: EMI 1C 137 53032-53036M LP: Arabesque 8107 CD: Pearl GEMMCD 9469 CD: Toshiba Shinseido SRG 1004 CD: Preiser 89202

Erlkönig (Wer reitet so spät durch Nacht und Wind?)

Berlin April 1939	Müller	78: Electrola DB 5523 78: Victor (Japan) ND 172/RL 66 LP: Rococo 5351 LP: World Records SHB 65 LP: Preiser LV 257 LP: Toshiba EAC 77365-77368 LP: Arabesque 8107 CD: Toshiba Shinseido SRG 1004 CD: Preiser 89017

Hüsch

Schubert Lieder/continued

Erstarrung/Winterreise (Ich such' im Schnee vergebens)

London April 1933	Müller	78: HMV DA 1344 78: Victor (Japan) JI 50/NFB 1 LP: Victor JF 1-2/LH 16 LP: Electrola E 80679-80680 LP: Preiser LV 203 LP: World Records SHB 65 LP: Toshiba HD 1032-1033/GR 2139-2140/ EAC 77365-77368 LP: EMI 1C 137 53032-53036M LP: Arabesque 8107 CD: Pearl GEMMCD 9469 CD: Toshiba Shinseido SRG 1004 CD: Preiser 89202

Das Fischermädchen/Schwanengesang (Du schönes Fischermädchen)

Berlin August 1937	Moore	HMV unpublished
London May 1938	Moore	LP: Rococo 5351 LP: Preiser LV 257 LP: Toshiba EAC 77365-77368 LP: Arabesque 8107 CD: Toshiba Shinseido SRG 1004 CD: Preiser 89017
Tokyo July 1952	Gurlitt	78: Victor (Japan) SF 718/JAS 249 LP: Victor (Japan) LS 103-104
Tokyo 1962	Kobayashi	LP: Victor (Japan) RA 2184 <u>Televised performance</u>

Frühlingssehnsucht/Schwanengesang (Säuselnde Lüfte wehend so mild)

Tokyo July 1952	Gurlitt	78: Victor (Japan) SD 3073/JAS 249 LP: Victor (Japan) LS 103-104
Tokyo 1952	Gurlitt	LP: King (Japan) K200 488 CD: King (Japan) K32Y 190
Tokyo 1962	Kobayashi	LP: Victor (Japan) RA 2184 <u>Televised performance</u>

Schubert Lieder/continued

Frühlingstraum/Winterreise (Ich träumte von bunten Blumen)

London April 1933	Müller	HMV unpublished
Berlin August 1933	Müller	78: HMV DB 2041 78: Victor (Japan) JD 359/NDB 3 45: Victor (Japan) EK 1010 LP: Victor JF 1-2/LH 16 LP: Electrola E 80679-80680 LP: Preiser LV 203 LP: World Records SHB 65 LP: Toshiba HD 1032-1033/GR 2139-2140/ EAC 77365-77368 LP: EMI 1C 137 53032-53036M LP: Arabesque 8107 CD: Pearl GEMMCD 9469 CD: Toshiba Shinseido SRG 1004 CD: Preiser 89202

Ganymed (Wie im Morgenglanze du rings mich anglühst)

Tokyo 1962	Mitsuishi	LP: Victor (Japan) RA 2189 <u>Televised performance</u>

Gefror'ne Tränen/Winterreise (Gefror'ne Tränen fallen von meinen Wangen ab)

London April 1933	Müller	HMV unpublished
Berlin August 1933	Müller	78: HMV DB 2039 78: Victor (Japan) JD 357/NDB 1 45: Victor (Japan) EK 1010 LP: Victor JF 1-2/LH 16 LP: Electrola E 80679-80680 LP: Preiser LV 203 LP: World Records SHB 65 LP: Toshiba HD 1032-1033/GR 2139-2140/ EAC 77365-77368 LP: EMI 1C 137 53032-53036M LP: Arabesque 8107 CD: Pearl GEMMCD 9469 CD: Toshiba Shinseido SRG 1004 CD: Preiser 89202

Schubert Lieder/continued

Der greise Kopf/Winterreise (Der Reif hatt' einen weissen Schein)

London April 1933	Müller	78: HMV DB 2042 78: Victor (Japan) JD 360/NDB 4 45: Victor (Japan) EK 14 LP: Victor JF 1-2/LH 16 LP: Electrola E 80679-80680 LP: Preiser LV 203 LP: World Records SHB 65 LP: Toshiba HD 1032-1033/GR 2139-2140/ EAC 77365-77368 LP: EMI 1C 137 53032-53036M LP: Arabesque 8107 CD: Pearl GEMMCD 9469 CD: Toshiba Shinseido SRG 1004 CD: Preiser 89202

Gute Nacht/Winterreise (Fremd bin ich eingezogen)

London April 1933	Müller	HMV unpublished
Berlin August 1933	Müller	78: HMV DB 2039 78: Victor (Japan) JD 357/NDB 1 45: Victor (Japan) EK 14 LP: Victor JF 1-2/LH 16 LP: Electrola E 80679-80680 LP: Preiser LV 203 LP: World Records SHB 65 LP: Toshiba HD 1032-1033/GR 2139-2140/ EAC 77365-77368 LP: EMI 1C 137 53032-53036M LP: Arabesque 8107 CD: Pearl GEMMCD 9469 CD: Toshiba Shinseido SRG 1004 CD: Preiser 89202
Berlin September 1933	Müller	HMV unpublished
Tokyo 1952	Gurlitt	LP: King (Japan) K200 488 CD: King (Japan) K32Y 190

Schubert Lieder/continued

Halt!/Die schöne Müllerin (Eine Mühle seh' ich blinken aus der Erlen heraus)

London January 1935	Müller	78: HMV DB 2429/DB 7828 78: Victor (Japan) JD 724/ND 198 LP: Victor (Japan) LT 110 LP: Electrola E 80685 LP: Angel DTX 20036 LP: Preiser LV 204 LP: World Records SH 295 LP: Melodiya D030911-030912 LP: Toshiba GR 2156/EAC 77365-77368 LP: Arabesque 8107 CD: Pearl GEMMCD 9479 CD: Toshiba Shinseido SRG 1004 CD: Preiser 89202

Horch', horch', die Lerch'!

Berlin April 1939	Müller	78: Electrola DB 5522 LP: Preiser LV 257 LP: World Records SHB 65 LP: Toshiba EAC 77365-77368 LP: Arabesque 8107 CD: Toshiba Shinseido SRG 1004 CD: Preiser 89017
Tokyo 1962	Mitsuishi	LP: Victor (Japan) RA 2189 <u>Televised performance</u>

Ihr Bild/Schwanengesang (Ich stand in dunklen Träumen)

Tokyo July 1952	Gurlitt	78: Victor (Japan) SF 717/JAS 249 LP: Victor (Japan) LS 103-104
Tokyo 1952	Gurlitt	LP: King (Japan) K200 488 CD: King (Japan) K32Y 190
Tokyo 1962	Kobayashi	LP: Victor (Japan) RA 2184 <u>Televised performance</u>

Schubert Lieder/continued

Im Dorfe/Winterreise (Es bellen die Hunde, es rasseln die Ketten)

London April 1933	Müller	78: HMV DB 2043 78: Victor (Japan) JD 361/NDB 5 45: Victor (Japan) EK 14 LP: Victor JF 1-2/LH 16 LP: Electrola E 80679-80680 LP: Preiser LV 203 LP: World Records SHB 65 LP: Toshiba HD 1032-1033/GR 2139-2140/ EAC 77365-77368 LP: EMI 1C 137 53032-53036M LP: Arabesque 8107 CD: Pearl GEMMCD 9469 CD: Toshiba Shinseido SRG 1004 CD: Preiser 89202

In der Ferne/Schwanengesang (Wehe den Fliehenden, Welt hinaus Ziehenden!)

Tokyo July 1952	Gurlitt	78: Victor (Japan) SD 3074/JAS 249 LP: Victor (Japan) LS 103-104
Tokyo 1962	Kobayashi	LP: Victor (Japan) RA 2184 Televised performance

Irrlicht/Winterreise (In die tiefsten Felsengründe)

London April 1933	Müller	HMV unpublished
Berlin August 1933	Müller	78: HMV DB 2041 78: Victor (Japan) JD 359/NDB 3 LP: Victor JF 1-2/LH 16 LP: Electrola E 80679-80680 LP: Preiser LV 203 LP: World Records SHB 65 LP: Toshiba HD 1032-1033/GR 2139-2140/ EAC 77365-77368 LP: EMI 1C 137 53032-53036M LP: Arabesque 8107 CD: Pearl GEMMCD 9469 CD: Toshiba Shinseido SRG 1004 CD: Preiser 89202

Schubert Lieder/continued

Der Jäger/Die schöne Müllerin (Was sucht denn der Jäger am Mühlbach hier?)

London January 1935	Müller	78: HMV DB 2434/DB 7830 78: Victor (Japan) JD 729/ND 203 LP: Victor (Japan) LT 110 LP: Electrola E 80685 LP: Angel DTX 20036 LP: Preiser LV 204 LP: World Records SH 295 LP: Melodiya D030911-030912 LP: Toshiba GR 2156/EAC 77365-77368 LP: Arabesque 8107 CD: Pearl GEMMCD 9479 CD: Toshiba Shinseido SRG 1004 CD: Preiser 89202
London February 1935	Müller	HMV unpublished

Die Krähe/Winterreise (Eine Krähe war mit mir aus der Stadt gezogen)

London April 1933	Müller	78: HMV DB 2042 78: Victor (Japan) JD 360/NDB 4 LP: Victor JF 1-2/LH 16 LP: Electrola E 80679-80680 LP: Preiser LV 203 LP: World Records SHB 65 LP: Toshiba HD 1032-1033/GR 2139-2140/ EAC 77365-77368 LP: EMI 1C 137 53032-53036M LP: Arabesque 8107 CD: Pearl GEMMCD 9469 CD: Toshiba Shinseido SRG 1004 CD: Preiser 89202
Tokyo 1952	Gurlitt	LP: King (Japan) K20O 488 CD: King (Japan) K32Y 190

Kriegers Ahnung/Schwanengesang (In tiefer Ruh' liegt um mich her)

Tokyo July 1952	Gurlitt	78: Victor (Japan) SD 3073/JAS 249 LP: Victor (Japan) LS 103-104
Tokyo 1962	Kobayashi	LP: Victor (Japan) RA 2184 **Televised performance**

Hüsch

Schubert Lieder/continued

Der Leiermann/Winterreise (Drüben hinterm Dorfe steht ein Leiermann)

London April 1933	Müller	HMV unpublished
Berlin August 1933	Müller	78: HMV DA 1346 78: Victor (Japan) JI 52/NFB 3 45: Victor (Japan) EK 1010 LP: Victor JF 1-2/LH 16 LP: Electrola E 80679-80680 LP: Preiser LV 203 LP: World Records SHB 65 LP: Toshiba HD 1032-1033/GR 2139-2140/ EAC 77365-77368 LP: EMI 1C 137 53032-53036M LP: Arabesque 8107 CD: Pearl GEMMCD 9469 CD: Toshiba Shinseido SRG 1004 CD: Preiser 89202
Tokyo 1952	Gurlitt	LP: King (Japan) K200 488 CD: King (Japan) K32Y 190

Letzte Hoffnung/Winterreise (Hie und da ist an den Bäumen)

London April 1933	Müller	78: HMV DB 2042 78: Victor (Japan) JD 360/NDB 4 LP: Victor JF 1-2/LH 16 LP: Electrola E 80679-80680 LP: Preiser LV 203 LP: World Records SHB 65 LP: Toshiba HD 1032-1033/GR 2139-2140/ EAC 77365-77368 LP: EMI 1C 137 53032-53036M LP: Arabesque 8107 CD: Pearl GEMMCD 9469 CD: Toshiba Shinseido SRG 1004 CD: Preiser 89202

Schubert Lieder/continued

Die liebe Farbe/Die schöne Müllerin (In Grün will ich mich kleiden)

London February 1935	Müller	78: HMV DB 2434/DB 7830 78: Victor (Japan) JD 729/ND 200 LP: Victor (Japan) LI 110 LP: Electrola E 80685 LP: Angel DTX 20036 LP: Preiser LV 204 LP: World Records SH 295 LP: Melodiya D030911-030912 LP: Toshiba GR 2156/EAC 77365-77368 LP: Arabesque 8107 CD: Pearl GEMMCD 9479 CD: Toshiba Shinseido SRG 1004 CD: Preiser 89202

Liebesbotschaft/Schwanengesang (Rauschendes Bächlein, so silbern und hell)

Tokyo July 1952	Gurlitt	78: Victor (Japan) SF 715/JAS 249 LP: Victor (Japan) LS 103-104
Tokyo 1952	Gurlitt	LP: King (Japan) K200 488 CD: King (Japan) K32Y 190
Tokyo 1962	Kobayashi	LP: Victor (Japan) RA 2184 <u>Televised performance</u>

Liebeslauschen (Hier unten steht ein Ritter im hellen Mondenstrahl)

Berlin April 1939	Müller	78: Electrola DB 5522 LP: Preiser LV 257 LP: Toshiba EAC 77365-77368 LP: Arabesque 8107 CD: Toshiba Shinseido SRG 1004 CD: Preiser 89017
Tokyo 1962	Mitsuishi	LP: Victor (Japan) RA 2189 <u>Televised performance</u>

Schubert Lieder/continued

Lied eines Schiffers an die Dioskuren (Dioskuren, Zwillingsbrüder!)

Berlin January 1939	Müller	78: Electrola DA 4452 LP: Rococo 5351 LP: Preiser LV 257 LP: World Records SHB 65 LP: EMI RLS 766 LP: Toshiba EAC 77365-77368 CD: Toshiba Shinseido SRG 1004 CD: Preiser 89017 CD: EMI CHS 566 1542
Tokyo 1962	Mitsuishi	LP: Victor (Japan) RA 2189 <u>Televised performance</u>

Der Lindenbaum/Winterreise (Am Brunnen vor dem Tore)

London April 1933	Müller	HMV unpublished
Berlin August 1933	Müller	78: HMV DB 2040 78: Victor (Japan) NFB 2 45: Victor (Japan) EK 1010 LP: Victor JF 1-2/LH 16 LP: Electrola E 80679-80680 LP: Preiser LV 203 LP: World Records SHB 65 LP: Toshiba HD 1032-1033/GR 2139-2140/ EAC 77365-77368 LP: EMI 1C 137 53032-53036M LP: Arabesque 8107 CD: Pearl GEMMCD 9469 CD: Toshiba Shinseido SRG 1004 CD: Preiser 89202
Tokyo 1952	Gurlitt	LP: King (Japan) K200 488 CD: King (Japan) K32Y 190

Schubert Lieder/continued

Mein!/Die schöne Müllerin (Bächlein, lass dein Rauschen sein!)

London February 1935	Müller		78: HMV DB 2433/DB 7831 78: Victor (Japan) JD 728/ND 201 LP: Victor (Japan) LT 110 LP: Electrola E 80685 LP: Angel DTX 20036 LP: Preiser LV 204 LP: World Records SH 295 LP: Melodiya D030911-030912 LP: Toshiba GR 2156/EAC 77365-77368 LP: Arabesque 8107 CD: Pearl GEMMCD 9479 CD: Toshiba Shinseido SRG 1004 CD: Preiser 89202

Memnon (Den Tag hindurch nur einmal mag ich sprechen)

Berlin November 1942	Müller	Unpublished radio broadcast

Mit dem grünen Lautenbande/Die schöne Müllerin(Schad'um das schöne grüne Band)

London January 1935	Müller	78: HMV DB 2434/DB 7830 78: Victor (Japan) JD 729/ND 200 LP: Victor (Japan) LT 110 LP: Electrola E 80685 LP: Angel DTX 20036 LP: Preiser LV 204 LP: World Records SH 295 LP: Melodiya D030911-030912 LP: Toshiba GR 2156/EAC 77365-77368 LP: Arabesque 8107 CD: Pearl GEMMCD 9479 CD: Toshiba Shinseido SRG 1004 CD: Preiser 89202
London February 1935	Müller	HMV unpublished

Schubert Lieder/continued

Morgengruss/Die schöne Müllerin (Guten Morgen, schöne Müllerin!)

London January 1935	Müller	78: HMV DB 2431/DB 7830 78: Victor (Japan) JD 726/ND 203 LP: Victor (Japan) LT 110 LP: Electrola E 80685 LP: Angel DTX 20036 LP: Preiser LV 204 LP: World Records SH 295 LP: Melodiya D030911-030912 LP: Toshiba GR 2156/EAC 77365-77368 LP: Arabesque 8107 CD: Pearl GEMMCD 9479 CD: Toshiba Shinseido SRG 1004 CD: Preiser 89202
Berlin March 1935	Müller	HMV unpublished

Der Müller und das Bach/Die schöne Müllerin (Wo ein treues Herze in Liebe vergeht)

London February 1935	Müller	HMV unpublished
Berlin March 1935	Müller	78: HMV DB 2436/DB 7828 78: Victor (Japan) JD 731/ND 198 LP: Victor (Japan) LT 110 LP: Electrola E 80685 LP: Angel DTX 20036 LP: Preiser LV 204 LP: World Records SH 295 LP: Melodiya D030911-030912 LP: Toshiba GR 2156/EAC 77365-77368 LP: Arabesque 8107 CD: Pearl GEMMCD 9479 CD: Toshiba Shinseido SRG 1004 CD: Preiser 89202

Schubert Lieder/continued

Des Müllers Blumen/Die schöne Müllerin (Am Bach viel' kleine Blumen steh'n)

London January 1935	Müller	78: HMV DB 2432/DB 7831 78: Victor (Japan) JD 727/ND 201 LP: Victor (Japan) LT 110 LP: Electrola E 80685 LP: Angel DTX 20036 LP: Preiser LV 204 LP: World Records SH 295 LP: Melodiya D030911-030912 LP: Toshiba GR 2156/EAC 77365-77368 LP: Arabesque 8107 CD: Pearl GEMMCD 9479 CD: Toshiba Shinseido SRG 1004 CD: Preiser 89202

Der Musensohn (Durch Feld und Wald zu schweifen)

Berlin November 1934	Müller	78: Electrola EG 3201/JK 9 LP: Rococo 5351 LP: World Records SHB 65 LP: Preiser LV 257 LP: Toshiba EAC 77365-77368 LP: Arabesque 8107 CD: Toshiba Shinseido SRG 1004 CD: Preiser 89017

Mut!/Winterreise (Fliegt der Schnee mir ins Gesicht)

London April 1933	Müller	HMV unpublished
Berlin August 1933	Müller	78: HMV DB 2044 78: Victor (Japan) JD 362/NDB 6 LP: Victor JF 1-2/LH 16 LP: Electrola E 80679-80680 LP: Preiser LV 203 LP: World Records SHB 65 LP: Toshiba HD 1032-1033/GR 2139-2140/ EAC 77365-77368 LP: EMI 1C 137 53032-53036M LP: Arabesque 8107 CD: Pearl GEMMCD 9469 CD: Toshiba Shinseido SRG 1004 CD: Preiser 89202
Tokyo 1952	Gurlitt	LP: King (Japan) K200 488 CD: King (Japan) K32Y 190

Schubert Lieder/continued

Die Nebensonnen/Winterreise (Drei Sonnen sah ich am Himmel steh'n)

London April 1933	Müller	HMV unpublished
Berlin August 1933	Müller	78: HMV DB 2044 78: Victor (Japan) JD 362/NDB 6 LP: Victor (Japan) LT 110 LP: Electrola E 80685 LP: Angel DTX 20036 LP: Preiser LV 204 LP: Melodiya D030911-030912 LP: Toshiba GR 2156/EAC 77365-77368 LP: Arabesque 8107 CD: Pearl GEMMCD 9479 CD: Toshiba Shinseido SRG 1004 CD: Preiser 89202
Tokyo 1952	Gurlitt	LP: King (Japan) K200 488 CD: King (Japan) K32Y 190

Der Neugierige/Die schöne Müllerin (Ich frage keine Blume)

London January 1935	Müller	78: HMV DB 2430/DB 7829 78: Victor (Japan) JD 725/ND 204

Schubert Lieder/continued

Pause/Die schöne Müllerin (Meine Laute hab' ich gehängt an die Wand)

London January 1935	Müller	78: HMV DB 2433/DB 7831 78: Victor (Japan) JD 728/ND 201 LP: Victor (Japan) LT 110 LP: Electrola E 80685 LP: Angel DTX 20036 LP: Preiser LV 204 LP: World Records SH 295 LP: Melodiya D030911-030912 LP: Toshiba GR 2156/EAC 77365-77368 LP: Arabesque 8107 CD: Pearl GEMMCD 9479 CD: Toshiba Shinseido SRG 1004 CD: Preiser 89202

Die Post/Winterreise (Von der Strasse her ein Posthorn klingt)

London April 1933	Müller	78: HMV DB 2042 78: Victor (Japan) JD 360/NDB 3 45: Victor (Japan) EK 14 LP: Victor JF 1-2/LH 16 LP: Electrola E 80679-80680 LP: Preiser LV 203 LP: World Records SHB 65 LP: Toshiba HD 1032-1033/GR 2139-2140/ EAC 77365-77368 LP: EMI 1C 137 53032-53036M LP: Arabesque 8107 CD: Pearl GEMMCD 9469 CD: Toshiba Shinseido SRG 1004 CD: Preiser 89202
Tokyo 1952	Gurlitt	LP: King (Japan) K200 488 CD: King (Japan) K32Y 190

Prometheus (Bedecke deinen Himmel, Zeus!)

Berlin November 1944	Müller	Unpublished radio broadcast

86 Hüsch

Schubert Lieder/continued

Rast/Winterreise (Nun merk' ich erst, wie müd' ich bin)

London April 1933	Müller	78: HMV DA 1345 78: Victor (Japan) JI 51/NFB 2 LP: Victor JF 1-2/LH 16 LP: Electrola E 80679-80680 LP: Preiser LV 203 LP: World Records SHB 65 LP: Toshiba HD 1032-1033/GR 2139-2140/ EAC 77365-77368 LP: EMI 1C 137 53032-53036M LP: Arabesque 8107 CD: Pearl GEMMCD 9469 CD: Toshiba Shinseido SRG 1004 CD: Preiser 89202

Das Rosenband (Im Frühlingsgarten fand ich sie)

Tokyo July 1952	Gurlitt	78: Victor (Japan) SF 719/JAS 275 45: Victor (Japan) ES 8031 LP: Victor (Japan) LS 2006

Rückblick/Winterreise (Es brennt mir unter beiden Sohlen)

London April 1933	Müller	HMV unpublished
Berlin August 1933	Müller	78: HMV DB 2041 78: Victor (Japan) JD 359/NDB 3 LP: Victor JF 1-2/LH 16 LP: Electrola E 80679-80680 LP: Preiser LV 203 LP: World Records SHB 65 LP: Toshiba HD 1032-1033/GR 2139-2140/ EAC 77365-77368 LP: EMI 1C 137 53032-53036M LP: Arabesque 8107 CD: Pearl GEMMCD 9469 CD: Toshiba Shinseido SRG 1004 CD: Preiser 89202

Schubert Lieder/continued

Schäfers Klagelied (Da droben auf jedem Berge)

Tokyo 1962	Mitsuishi	LP: Victor (Japan) RA 2189 <u>Televised performance</u>

Die Stadt/Schwanengesang (Am fernen Horizonte)

Tokyo July 1952	Gurlitt	78: Victor (Japan) SF 718/JAS 249 LP: Victor (Japan) LS 103-104
Tokyo 1962	Kobayashi	LP: Victor (Japan) RA 2184 <u>Televised performance</u>

Ständchen/Schwanengesang (Leise flehen meine Lieder)

Berlin March 1938	Müller	78: Electrola DB 4445 LP: Rococo 5351 LP: Preiser LV 208
Tokyo July 1952	Gurlitt	78: Victor (Japan) SF 715/JAS 249 45: Victor (Japan) ES 8013 LP: Victor (Japan) LS 103-104
Tokyo 1952	Gurlitt	LP: King (Japan) K20O 488 CD: King (Japan) K32Y 190
Tokyo 1962	Kobayashi	LP: Victor (Japan) RA 2184 <u>Televised performance</u>

Schubert Lieder/continued

Der stürmische Morgen/Winterreise (Wie hat der Sturm zerrissen)

London April 1933	Müller	78: HMV DB 2043 78: Victor (Japan) JD 361/NDB 5 LP: Victor JF 1-2/LH 16 LP: Electrola E 80679-80680 LP: Preiser LV 203 LP: World Records SHB 65 LP: Toshiba HD 1032-1033/GR 2139-2140/ EAC 77365-77368 LP: EMI 1C 137 53032-53036M LP: Arabesque 8107 CD: Pearl GEMMCD 9469 CD: Toshiba Shinseido SRG 1004 CD: Preiser 89202
Tokyo 1952	Gurlitt	LP: King (Japan) K20C 488 CD: King (Japan) K32Y 190

Die Taubenpost/Schwanengesang (Ich hab' eine Brieftaub' in meinem Sold)

Berlin August 1937	Moore	LP: World Records SHB 65 LP: EMI RLS 766 LP: Toshiba EAC 77365-77368 LP: Arabesque 8107 CD: Toshiba Shinseido SRG 1004 CD: Preiser 89017 CD: EMI CHS 566 1542
Tokyo July 1952	Gurlitt	78: Victor (Japan) SD 3075/JAS 249 LP: Victor (Japan) LS 103-104
Tokyo 1952	Gurlitt	LP: King (Japan) K200 488 CD: King (Japan) K32Y 190
Tokyo 1962	Kobayashi	LP: Victor (Japan) RA 2184 **Televised performance**

Schubert Lieder/continued

Täuschung/Winterreise (Ein Licht tanzt freundlich vor mir her)

London April 1933	Müller	HMV unpublished

Berlin August 1933	Müller	78: HMV DA 1346 78: Victor (Japan) JI 52/NFB 3 LP: Victor JF 1-2/LH 16 LP: Electrola E 80679-80680 LP: Preiser LV 203 LP: World Records SHB 65 LP: Toshiba HD 1032-1033/GR 2139-2140/ EAC 77365-77368 LP: EMI 1C 137 53032-53036M LP: Arabesque 8107 CD: Pearl GEMMCD 9469 CD: Toshiba Shinseido SRG 1004 CD: Preiser 89202
Tokyo 1952	Gurlitt	LP: King (Japan) K200 488 CD: King (Japan) K32Y 190

Tränenregen/Die schöne Müllerin (Wir sassen so traulich beisammen)

London January 1935	Müller	78: HMV DB 2432/DB 7831 78: Victor (Japan) JD 727/ND 201 LP: Victor (Japan) LT 110 LP: Electrola E 80685 LP: Angel DTX 20036 LP: Preiser LV 204 LP: World Records SH 295 LP: Melodiya D030911-030912 LP: Toshiba GR 2156/EAC 77365-77368 LP: Arabesque 8107 CD: Pearl GEMMCD 9479 CD: Toshiba Shinseido SRG 1004 CD: Preiser 89202

Schubert Lieder/continued

Trock'ne Blumen/Die schöne Müllerin (Ihr Blümlein alle, die sie mir gab)

London	Müller	78: HMV DB 2435/DB 7829
February		78: Victor (Japan) JD 730/ND 199
1935		LP: Victor (Japan) LT 110
		LP: Electrola E 80685
		LP: Angel DTX 20036
		LP: Preiser LV 204
		LP: World Records SH 295
		LP: Melodiya D030911-030912
		LP: Toshiba GR 2156/EAC 77365-77368
		LP: Arabesque 8107
		CD: Pearl GEMMCD 9479
		CD: Toshiba Shinseido SRG 1004
		CD: Preiser 89202

Ungeduld/Die schöne Müllerin (Ich schnitt' es gern in alle Rinden ein)

London	Müller	78: HMV DB 2431/DB 7833
February		78: Victor (Japan) JD 726/ND 203
1935		45: Victor (Japan) EK 13
		LP: Victor (Japan) LT 110
		LP: Electrola E 80685
		LP: Angel DTX 20036
		LP: Preiser LV 204
		LP: World Records SH 295
		LP: Melodiya D030911-030912
		LP: Toshiba GR 2156/EAC 77365-77368
		LP: Arabesque 8107
		CD: Pearl GEMMCD 9479
		CD: Toshiba Shinseido SRG 1004
		CD: Preiser 89202

Der Wanderer (Ich komme vom Gebirge her)

Berlin	Müller	78: Electrola EG 3201/JK 9
November		LP: World Records SHB 65
1934		LP: Rococo 5351
		LP: Toshiba EAC 77365-77368
		LP: Arabesque 8107
		CD: Toshiba Shinseido SRG 1004

Schubert Lieder/continued

Das Wandern/Die schöne Müllerin (Das Wandern ist des Müllers Lust)

London January 1935	Müller	78: HMV DB 2429/DB 7828 78: Victor (Japan) JD 724/ND 198 45: Victor (Japan) EK 13 LP: Victor (Japan) LT 110 LP: Electrola E 80685 LP: Angel DTX 20036 LP: Preiser LV 204 LP: World Records SH 295 LP: Melodiya D030911-030912 LP: Toshiba GR 2156/EAC 77365-77368 LP: Arabesque 8107 CD: Pearl GEMMCD 9479 CD: Toshiba Shinseido SRG 1004 CD: Preiser 89202
Tokyo 1962	Mitsuishi	LP: Victor (Japan) RA 2189 <u>Televised performance</u>

Wasserflut/Winterreise (Manche Trän' aus meinen Augen)

London April 1933	Müller	HMV unpublished
Berlin August 1933	Müller	78: HMV DB 2040 78: Victor (Japan) JD 358/NDB 2 LP: Victor JF 1-2/LH 16 LP: Electrola E 80679-80680 LP: Preiser LV 203 LP: World Records SHB 65 LP: Toshiba HD 1032-1033/GR 2139-2140/ EAC 77365-77368 LP: EMI 1C 137 53032-53036M LP: Arabesque 8107 CD: Pearl GEMMCD 9469 CD: Toshiba Shinseido SRG 1004 CD: Preiser 89202

Schubert Lieder/continued

Der Wegweiser/Winterreise (Was vermeid' ich denn die Wege)

London April 1933	Müller	78: HMV DB 2043 78: Victor (Japan) JD 361/NDB 5 LP: Victor JF 1-2/LH 16 LP: Electrola E 80679-80680 LP: Preiser LV 203 LP: World Records SHB 65 LP: Toshiba HD 1032-1033/GR 2139-2140/ EAC 77365-77368 LP: EMI 1C 137 53032-53036M LP: Arabesque 8107 CD: Pearl GEMMCD 9469 CD: Toshiba Shinseido SRG 1004 CD: Preiser 89202
Tokyo 1952	Gurlitt	LP: King (Japan) K200 488 CD: King (Japan) K32Y 190

Wer nie sein Brot mit Tränen ass/Gesänge des Harfners

Berlin January 1939	Müller	78: Electrola DB 5524 LP: Electrola E 83393 LP: World Records SHB 65 LP: Preiser LV 105 LP: Toshiba EAC 77365-77368 LP: Arabesque 8107 CD: Toshiba Shinseido SRG 1004 CD: Preiser 89017

Wer sich der Einsamkeit ergibt/Gesänge des Harfners

Berlin January 1939	Müller	78: Electrola DB 5524 LP: Electrola E 83393 LP: World Records SHB 65 LP: Preiser LV 105 LP: Toshiba EAC 77365-77368 LP: Arabesque 8107 CD: Toshiba Shinseido SRG 1004 CD: Preiser 89017

Schubert Lieder/continued

Die Wetterfahne/Winterreise (Der Wind spielt mit der Wetterfahne)

London April 1933	Müller	HMV unpublished
Berlin August 1933	Müller	78: HMV DB 2039 78: Victor (Japan) JD 357/NDB 1 LP: Victor JF 1-2/LH 16 LP: Electrola E 80679-80680 LP: Preiser LV 203 LP: World Records SHB 65 LP: Toshiba HD 1032-1033/GR 2139-2140/ EAC 77365-77368 LP: EMI 1C 137 53032-53036M LP: Arabesque 8107 CD: Pearl GEMMCD 9469 CD: Toshiba Shinseido SRG 1004 CD: Preiser 89202

Widerschein (Harrt ein Fischer auf der Brücke)

Berlin January 1939	Müller	78: Electrola DA 4452 LP: World Records SHB 65 LP: Rococo 5351 LP: Preiser LV 257 LP: Toshiba EAC 77365-77368 LP: EMI RLS 766 LP: Arabesque 8107 CD: Toshiba Shinseido SRG 1004 CD: Preiser 89017 CD: EMI CHS 566 1542

Das Wirtshaus/Winterreise (Auf einen Totenacker hat mich mein Weg gebracht)

London April 1933	Müller	78: HMV DB 2044 78: Victor (Japan) JD 362/NDB 6 LP: Victor JF 1-2/LH 16 LP: Electrola E 80679-80680 LP: Preiser LV 203 LP: World Records SHB 65 LP: Toshiba HD 1032-1033/GR 2139-2140/ EAC 77365-77368 LP: EMI 1C 137 53032-53036M LP: Arabesque 8107 CD: Pearl GEMMCD 9469 CD: Toshiba Shinseido SRG 1004 CD: Preiser 89202

Schubert Lieder/concluded

Wohin?/Die schöne Müllerin (Ich hört' ein Bächlein rauschen)

London	Müller	78: HMV DB 2429/DB 7828
January		78: Victor (Japan) JD 724/ND 198
1935		45: Victor (Japan) EK 13
		LP: Victor (Japan) LT 110
		LP: Electrola E 80685
		LP: Angel DTX 20036
		LP: Preiser LV 204
		LP: World Records SH 295
		LP: Melodiya D030911-030912
		LP: Toshiba GR 2156/EAC 77365-77368
		LP: Arabesque 8107
		CD: Pearl GEMMCD 9479
		CD: Toshiba Shinseido SRG 1004
		CD: Preiser 89202

ROBERT SCHUMANN (1810-1856)

Allnächtlich im Traume/Dichterliebe

London January 1936	Müller	78: HMV DB 2940/DB 8227 78: Victor (Japan) JAS 217 LP: Victor GNR 109 LP: Preiser LV 105 LP: Arabesque 8136 CD: Pearl GEMMCDS 9119

Die alten bösen Lieder/Dichterliebe

London January 1936	Müller	78: HMV DB 2942/DB 8227 78: Victor (Japan) JAS 217 LP: Victor GNR 109 LP: Preiser LV 105 LP: Arabesque 8136 CD: Pearl GEMMCDS 9119

Am leuchtenden Sommermorgen/Dichterliebe

London January 1936	Müller	78: HMV DB 2941/DB 8229 78: Victor (Japan) JAS 217 LP: Victor GNR 109 LP: Preiser LV 105 LP: Arabesque 8136 CD: Pearl GEMMCDS 9119

Aus alten Märchen winkt es/Dichterliebe

London January 1936	Müller	78: HMV DB 2942/DB 8228 78: Victor JAS 217 LP: Victor GNR 109 LP: Preiser LV 105 LP: Arabesque 8136 CD: Pearl GEMMCDS 9119

Schumann Lieder/continued

Aus meinen Tränen spriessen/Dichterliebe

London	Müller	78: HMV DB 2940/DB 8227
January		78: Victor (Japan) JAS 217
1936		LP: Victor GNR 109
		LP: Preiser LV 105
		LP: Arabesque 8136
		CD: Pearl GEMMCDS 9119

Die beiden Grenadiere (Nach Frankreich zogen zwei Grenadier')

Berlin	Staatskapelle	78: Parlophone R 972
October	Weissmann	78: Parlophone (Australia) A 3244
1930		78: Odeon O-25932
		78: Decca (USA) 20021
		78: Columbia (Japan) J 5362/P 24/38781

Das ist ein Flöten und Geigen/Dichterliebe

London	Müller	78: HMV DB 2941/DB 8229
January		78: Victor (Japan) JAS 217
1936		LP: Victor GNR 109
		LP: Preiser LV 105
		LP: Arabesque 8136
		CD: Pearl GEMMCDS 9119

Hör' ich das Liedchen klingen/Dichterliebe

London	Müller	78: HMV DB 2941/DB 8229
January		78: Victor (Japan) JAS 217
1936		LP: Victor GNR 109
		LP: Arabesque 8136
		CD: Pearl GEMMCDS 9119

Ich grolle nicht/Dichterliebe

London	Müller	78: HMV DB 2940/DB 8228
January		78: Victor (Japan) JAS 217
1936		LP: Victor GNR 109
		LP: Preiser LV 105
		LP: Arabesque 8136
		CD: Pearl GEMMCDS 9119

Schumann Lieder/continued

Ich hab' im Traum geweinet/Dichterliebe

London January 1936	Müller	78: HMV DB 2941/DB 8229 78: Victor (Japan) JAS 217 LP: Victor GNR 109 LP: Preiser LV 105 LP: Arabesque 8136 CD: Pearl GEMMCDS 9119

Ich will meine Seele tauchen/Dichterliebe

London January 1936	Müller	78: HMV DB 2940/DB 8228 78: Victor (Japan) JAS 217 LP: Victor GNR 109 LP: Preiser LV 105 LP: Arabesque 8136 CD: Pearl GEMMCDS 9119

Im Rhein, im heiligen Strome/Dichterliebe

London January 1936	Müller	78: HMV DB 2940/DB 8228 78: Victor (Japan) JAS 217 LP: Victor GNR 109 LP: Preiser LV 105 LP: Arabesque 8136 CD: Pearl GEMMCDS 9119

Im wunderschönen Monat Mai/Dichterliebe

London January 1936	Müller	78: HMV DB 2940/DB 8227 78: Victor (Japan) JAS 217 LP: Victor GNR 109 LP: Preiser LV 105 LP: Arabesque 8136 CD: Pearl GEMMCDS 9119

Ein Jüngling liebt ein Mädchen/Dichterliebe

London January 1936	Müller	78: HMV DB 2941/DB 8229 78: Victor (Japan) JAS 217 LP: Victor GNR 109 LP: Preiser LV 105 LP: Arabesque 8136 CD: Pearl GEMMCDS 9119

Schumann Lieder/concluded

Mondnacht/Liederkreis op 39 (Es war, als hätt' der Himmel)

Berlin   Müller   Electrola unpublished
January
1936

Der Nussbaum (Es grünet ein Nussbaum vor dem Haus)

Berlin   Müller   Electrola unpublished
January
1936

Die Rose, die Lilie, die Taube/Dichterliebe

London   Müller   78: HMV DB 2940/DB 8227
January   78: Victor (Japan) JAS 217
1936   LP: Victor GNR 109
                                    LP: Preiser LV 105
                                    LP: Arabesque 8136
                                    CD: Pearl GEMMCDS 9119

Und wüssten's die Blumen/Dichterliebe

London   Müller   78: HMV DB 2941/DB 8229
January   78: Victor (Japan) JAS 217
1936   LP: Victor GNR 109
                                    LP: Preiser LV 105
                                    LP: Arabesque 8136
                                    CD: Pearl GEMMCDS 9119

Wenn ich in deine Augen seh'/Dichterliebe

London   Müller   78: HMV DB 2940/DB 8227
January   78: Victor (Japan) JAS 217
1936   LP: Victor GNR 109
                                    LP: Preiser LV 105
                                    LP: Arabesque 8136
                                    CD: Pearl GEMMCDS 9119

JOHANN STRAUSS (1825-1899)

Die Fledermaus

Berlin August 1936	Role of Falke Eipperle, Beilke, Fidesser, Reinmar, Marischka Reichssender Orchestra & Chorus Hainisch	Unpublished radio broadcast

Die Fledermaus, unspecified extracts

Berlin February 1934	Role of Falke Berger, Pfahl, Heindl, Reinmar, Wörle Staatskapelle and Chorus Müller	Untraced radio broadcast

RICHARD STRAUSS (1864-1949)

Arabella, excerpt (So wie Sie sind)

Berlin December 1940	Lemnitz Staatskapelle Seidler-Winkler	78: Electrola DB 5606 LP: Electrola E 83393 LP: Rococo 5203 LP: Preiser LV 160 LP: World Records SHB 47 LP: Eterna 820.898 LP: Toshiba EAC 77365-77368 LP: EMI 1C 137 46347-46348M/ 1C 147 28989-28990M CD: ZYX Music PD 50182

Arabella, excerpt (Das war sehr gut, Mandryka!)

Berlin 1943	Lemnitz Städtische Oper Orchestra Grüber	LP: Rococo 5300 LP: Eterna 820 898 LP: Historia H 704-705 LP: BASF 22 1776/22 177/22 22110-5 CD: Berlin Classics BC 90142 Some issues name conductor as Rother

100 Hüsch

Du meines Herzens Krönelein

Tokyo July 1952	Gurlitt	78: Victor (Japan) SF 721/JAS 275 LP: Victor (Japan) LS 2006

Morgen (Und morgen wird die Sonne wieder scheinen)

Tokyo July 1952	Gurlitt	78: Victor (Japan) SF 721/JAS 275

Traum durch die Dämmerung (Weite Wiesen im Dämmergrau)

Tokyo July 1952	Gurlitt	78: Victor (Japan) SF 725 LP: Victor (Japan) LS 2006

Zueignung (Ja, du weisst es, teure Seele!)

Berlin May 1934	Orchestra Dobrindt	78: Electrola EG 3056 LP: Preiser LV 76
Tokyo July 1952	Gurlitt	78: Victor (Japan) SF 725 LP: Victor (Japan) LS 2006

AMBROISE THOMAS (1811-1896)

Mignon, excerpt (De son coeur)

Berlin September 1937	Staatskapelle Müller <u>Sung in German</u>	78: Electrola EG 6136/JK 2607 LP: Rococo 5351 LP: Preiser LV 285 CD: Preiser 89071

GIUSEPPE VERDI (1813-1901)

Aida, excerpt (Aida! Tu non m'ami!/Ma, dimmi, per qual via?)

Berlin November 1934	Teschemacher, Wittrisch Staatskapelle Blech Sung in German	78: Electrola DB 4431 LP: Preiser LV 286 LP: Historia H 663-664 LP: Club 99-57

Un ballo in maschera, excerpt (Alla vita che t' arride)

Berlin December 1940	Staatskapelle Müller Sung in German	78: Electrola DA 4488 LP: Rococo 5248

Un ballo in maschera, excerpt (Eri tu)

Berlin October 1937	Staatskapelle Müller Sung in German	78: Electrola DB 4510 CD: Preiser 89071

La forza del destino, excerpt (Solenne in quest' ora)

Berlin August 1932	Groh Orchestra Dobrindt	78: Parlophone B 48229/B 49758/R 1757 78: Parlophone (Australia) A 3624 78: Odeon O-25107/O-11990/O-6950 CD: Pearl GEMMCD 9419
Berlin October 1937	Rosvaenge Staatskapelle Seidler-Winkler Sung in German	78: Electrola DB 4499 LP: Rococo 5247 CD: Pearl GEMMCD 9394 CD: Grammofono AB 78668-78669

Otello, excerpt (Era la notte)

Berlin April 1930	Staatskapelle Weissmann Sung in German	78: Parlophone B 12455/R 979 78: Parlophone (Australia) A 3286 78: Odeon O-25093 78: Decca (USA) 20036 LP: Rococo 5248 LP: Preiser LV 285

102   Hüsch

Rigoletto, excerpt (Pari siamo)

Berlin April 1930	Staatskapelle Weissmann <u>Sung in German</u>	78: Parlophone P 9550/E 11034 78: Odeon O-7792
Berlin February 1938	Staatskapelle Müller <u>Sung in German</u>	78: Electrola DB 4539

Rigoletto, excerpt (Cortigiani, vil razza!)

Berlin April 1930	Staatskapelle Weissmann <u>Sung in German</u>	78: Parlophone P 9550/E 11034 78: Odeon O-7792
Berlin February 1938	Staatskapelle Müller <u>Sung in German</u>	78: Electrola DB 4539

Rigoletto, excerpt (Solo per me l'infamia)

Berlin May 1937	Perras Staatskapelle Seidler-Winkler <u>Sung in German</u>	Electrola unpublished

La traviata, Querschnitt

Berlin November 1935	Perras, W.Ludwig Staatskapelle Seidler-Winkler <u>Sung in German</u>	78: Electrola EH 930/FX 181 45: Electrola 7PW 550

La traviata, excerpt (Dite alle giovine)

Berlin May 1937	Perras Staatskapelle Seidler-Winkler Sung in German	Electrola unpublished

La traviata, excerpt (Di provenza il mar)

Berlin October 1928	Staatskapelle Weissmann Sung in German	78: Parlophone E 11091 78: Parlophone (Australia) A 4323
Berlin November 1932	Orchestra Dobrindt Sung in German	78: Parlophone B 49758 78: Odeon O-11990
Berlin December 1940	Staatskapelle Müller Sung in German	78: Electrola DA 4488

Il trovatore, excerpt (Per me ora fatale)

Berlin June 1932	Orchestra and Chorus Weissmann Sung in German	78: Parlophone B 48219 78: Odeon O-25095
Berlin March 1935	Strienz Staatskapelle Müller Sung in German	78: Electrola EH 917 78: Victor (Japan) JH 188 LP: Preiser LV 285 Includes recitative beginning Qual suono

Il trovatore, excerpt (Tutto è deserto/Il balen del suo sorriso)

Berlin March 1935	Strienz Staatskapelle Müller Sung in German	78: Electrola EH 917 78: Victor (Japan) JH 188 LP: Rococo 5248 LP: Preiser LV 285 CD: Preiser 89071
Frankfurt May 1935	Frankfurt RO Rosbaud Sung in German	Untraced radio broadcast

Städtisches Opernhaus-Restaurant
Inhaber Hermann Lindner

 Theatersoupers zu zeitgemäßen Preisen
In allen Räumen Bier
Gesellschaftszimmer und Festsäle

Fernsprecher: C4 Wilhelm 0793

Turnus III

Dienstag, den 21. März 1933

DON GIOVANNI

Heiteres Drama in 2 Aufzügen (10 Bildern) von Lorenzo da Ponte. Textbearbeitung von Hermann Levi. Durchgesehen und herausgegeben von Dr. Otto Erhardt

Musik von Wolfgang Amadeus Mozart
Musikalische Leitung: Werner Ladwig
Gesamtausstattung: Professor Max Slevogt

Kassenöffnung 18½ (6½) Uhr   Anfang 19½ (7½) Uhr
Ende gegen 23 (11) Uhr

Das Fundbüro der Städt. Oper, Erdgeschoß (Zimmer 23), Eingang Sesenheimer Straße, ist werktags von 10—2 Uhr geöffnet

Eigener Untergrundbahnhof mit direktem Eingang zur Städtischen Oper

---

Don Giovanni	Gerhard Hüsch
Der Komtur	Carl Braun a. G.
Donna Anna, seine Tochter	Nelly Merz a. G.
Don Oktavio, ihr Verlobter	Walther Ludwig
Donna Elvira	Rosalind von Schirach
Leporello, Diener des Don Giovanni	Anton Baumann
Masetto, ein Bauer	Edwin Heyer
Zerlina, seine Braut	Irene Eisinger
Eine Zofe	Margot Höpfner

Bauern, Bäuerinnen, Spielleiter, Diener

Ort der Handlung: Eine spanische Stadt

In Vorbereitung:

Der Waffenschmied

von Albert Lortzing

Dirigent: Hanns Udo Müller
Inszenierung: Otto Krauss
Bühnenbild: Gustav Vargo

G. BARGENDE
K.-G.

TEPPICHE
LINOLEUM
Läuferstoffe · Tisch- und Divandecken · Belegen von Flächen und Treppen

Charlottenburg 5, Kaiserdamm 3 und
Windscheidstr. 11 · C4 Wilhelm 7640

---

25. März 1933
Hausball der Städtischen Oper
mit Nachtvorstellung

Bühnenfestspiele Bayreuth

Dienstag, den 21. Juli 1931

TANNHÄUSER
und der Sängerkrieg auf Wartburg

Orchesterleitung: **Arturo Toscanini** Gesamtinszenierung: **Siegfried Wagner**
Chöre: **Hugo Rüdel** Technische Leitung: **Friedrich Kranich**
Choreographie: **Rudolf von Laban**
Solostudium: **Carl Kittel** Kostüme: **Daniela Thode**
Spielleitung: **Alexander Spring**

Personen:

Hermann, Landgraf von Thüringen		Ivar Andrésen
Tannhäuser		Lauritz Melchior
Wolfram von Eschenbach		Gerhard Hüsch
Walter von der Vogelweide	Ritter und Sänger	Gustav Rödin
Biterolf		Georg von Tschurtschenthaler
Heinrich der Schreiber		Joachim Sattler
Reinmar von Zweter		Dezsö Ernster
Elisabeth, Nichte des Landgrafen		Maria Müller
Venus		Anny Helm
Ein junger Hirte		Erna Berger

Thüringische Grafen und Edelleute. Edelfrauen. Edelknaben. Aeltere und jüngere Pilger.

Bacchanal

Dramatischer Entwurf: **Siegfried Wagner**
Choreographische Einstudierung: **Rudolf von Laban**

Die 3 Grazien	Trude Hillinger-Pohl / Herta Feist / Elsa Kahl-Cohen
Erste Bacchantin	Inge Herting

Bacchantinnen, Nymphen, Jünglinge, Faune: Tänzerinnen und Tänzer aus dem Kreis **Rudolf von Labans**

1. Aufzug: Das Innere des Hörselberges bei Eisenach; ein Tal vor der Wartburg.
2. Aufzug: Auf der Wartburg. 3. Aufzug: Tal vor der Wartburg. Im Anfange des 13. Jahrhunderts.

Dekorations-Entwürfe von Siegfried Wagner und Curt Söhnlein.
Der Venusberg ist den Feengrotten in Saalfeld nachgebildet.

Nachdruck verboten
Für die Besetzung ist nur das im Festspielhaus ausgegebene Tagesprogramm verbindlich

Bayreuther Festspielführer 1931 im Einvernehmen mit der Festspielleitung herausgegeben vom Verlag der Buchhandlung Georg Niehrenheim, Bayreuth. Vorrätig im Kiosk am Festspielhause, sowie in allen Buchhandlungen und in den Schreibwarengeschäften. — Preis Mk. 4.50.

Hüsch

VITZTHUM

Das Hakenkreuz

Berlin	Berlin SO	78: Telefunken E 1381
1932	F.A.Schmidt	

RICHARD WAGNER (1813-1883)

Tannhäuser, excerpt (Als du in kühnem Sange)

Berlin	Staatskapelle	78: Electrola EH 1003
August	Müller	78: Victor (Japan) JD 1274/ND 725
1936		LP: Arabesque 8022
		CD: EMI CMS 764 0082

Tannhäuser, excerpt (Blick' ich umher in diesem edlen Kreise)

Berlin	Staatskapelle	78: Parlophone P 9379/E 11046
December	Weissmann	78: Parlophone (Australia) A 4280
1928		78: Odeon O-7735
		78: Decca (USA) 25443
		CD: Pearl GEMMCDS 9121

Berlin	Staatskapelle	78: Electrola EH 983
August	Müller	78: HMV DB 4049
1936		78: Victor (Japan) JD 1143/ND 669
		LP: Preiser LV 285
		LP: Arabesque 8022
		CD: Preiser 89071

Tannhäuser, excerpt (Wohl wusst' ich hier sie im Gebet zu finden)

Berlin October– December 1928	Staatskapelle Weissmann	78: Parlophone E 10839 78: Parlophone (Australia) A 4138 78: Decca (USA) 25106
Berlin August 1936	Staatskapelle Müller	78: Electrola EH 1003 78: Victor (Japan) JD 1274/ND 725 LP: EMI 1C 181 30669-30678M/ RLS 7711/EX 29 02123 CD: EMI CMS 764 0082

Tannhäuser, excerpt (Wie Todesahnung/O du mein holder Abendstern)

Berlin December 1928	Staatskapelle Weissmann	78: Parlophone P 9379/E 10839 78: Parlophone (Australia) A 4138 78: Odeon O-7335 78: Decca (USA) 25106 CD: Nimbus NI 7867
Berlin August 1936	Staatskapelle Müller	78: Electrola EH 983 78: HMV DB 4049 78: Victor (Japan) JD 1143/ND 669 LP: Preiser LV 285 LP: EMI RLS 7711/EX 29 02123 CD: Pearl GEMMCDS 9121 CD: Preiser 89071 CD: Musica memoria 30283

CARL MARIA VON WEBER (1786–1826)

Der Freischütz

Berlin December 1936	Role of Ottokar Lemnitz, Beilke, Wittrisch, Bohnen, Böhme Berlin RO and Chorus Steiner	Unpublished radio broadcast

HUGO WOLF (1860-1903)

Anakreons Grab/Goethe-Lieder (Wo die Rose hier blüht)

Tokyo July 1952	Gurlitt	78: Victor (Japan) SD 3091 LP: Victor (Japan) LS 2006

Auf dem grünen Balkon/Spanisches Liederbuch

Berlin October 1934	Müller	HMV unpublished
Berlin November 1934	Müller	HMV unpublished
London February 1935	Müller	78: HMV DB 2703 LP: EMI RLS 759/1C 163 03991-03997M CD: Pearl GEMMCDS 9085

Benedeit die sel'ge Mutter/Italienisches Liederbuch

Berlin October 1932	Bos	78: HMV DB 2049 LP: EMI RLS 759/1C 163 03991-03997M CD: Pearl GEMMCDS 9075

Dass doch gemalt all' deine Reize wären/Italienisches Liederbuch

Berlin September 1934	Müller	78: HMV DB 2372 LP: Electrola E 83393 LP: EMI RLS 759/1C 163 03991-03997M CD: Pearl GEMMCDS 9085

Epiphanias/Goethe-Lieder (Die heil'gen drei Könige)

Berlin October 1932	Bos	78: HMV DB 1827 LP: EMI RLS 759/1C 163 03991-03997M CD: Pearl GEMMCDS 9075

Wolf Lieder/continued

Fussreise/Mörike-Lieder (Am frischgeschnitt'nen Wanderstab)

Tokyo July 1952	Gurlitt	78: Victor (Japan) SF 720/JAS 275 45: Victor (Japan) ES 8031

Genialisch Treiben/Goethe-Lieder (So wälz' ich ohne Unterlass)

Berlin October 1932	Bos	78: HMV DB 1827 LP: EMI RLS 759/1C 163 03991-03997M CD: Pearl GEMMCDS 9075

Gesang Weylas/Mörike-Lieder (Du bist Orplid, mein Land!)

Tokyo July 1952	Gurlitt	78: Victor (Japan) SD 3091 LP: Victor (Japan) LS 2006

Gesegnet sei, durch den die Welt entstund/Italienisches Liederbuch

Berlin September 1934	Müller	HMV unpublished
Berlin October 1934	Müller	78: HMV DB 2371 LP: Electrola E 83393 LP: EMI RLS 759/1C 163 03991-03997M LP: Toohiba EAC 77365-77368 CD: Pearl GEMMCDS 9085

Heut' nacht erhob ich mich/Italienisches Liederbuch

Berlin September 1934	Müller	78: HMV DB 2372 LP: EMI RLS 759/1C 163 03991-03997M CD: Pearl GEMMCDS 9085

Wolf Lieder/continued

Hoffärtig seid ihr, schönes Kind/Italienisches Liederbuch

Berlin September 1934	Müller	HMV unpublished
Berlin October 1934	Müller	78: HMV DB 2371 LP: EMI RLS 759/1C 163 03991-03997M CD: Pearl GEMMCDS 9085

Ihr seid die allerschönste weit und breit/Italienisches Liederbuch

Berlin September 1934	Müller	HMV unpublished
Berlin October 1934	Müller	78: HMV DB 2371 LP: EMI RLS 759/1C 163 03991-03997M CD: Pearl GEMMCDS 9085

Der Knabe und das Immlein/Mörike-Lieder (Im Weinberg auf der Höhe)

Tokyo July 1952	Gurlitt	78: Victor (Japan) SF 720/JAS 275 45: Victor (Japan) ES 8031

Der Mond hat eine schwere Klag' erhoben/Italienisches Liederbuch

Berlin October 1932	Bos	78: HMV DB 2049 LP: EMI RLS 759/1C 163 03991-03997M CD: Pearl GEMMCDS 9075

Der Rattenfänger/Goethe-Lieder (Ich bin der wohlbekannte Sänger)

Berlin October 1932	Bos	78: HMV DB 1827 LP: EMI RLS 759/1C 163 03991-03997M CD: Pearl GEMMCDS 9075

Wolf Lieder/conctinued

Schon streckt' ich aus im Bett die müden Glieder/Italienisches Liederbuch

Berlin	Bos	78: HMV DB 2049
October		LP: EMI RLS 759/1C 163 03991-03997M
1932		CD: Pearl GEMMCDS 9075

Ein Ständchen euch zu bringen kam ich her/Italienisches Liederbuch

Berlin	Müller	78: HMV DB 2372
September		LP: EMI RLS 759/1C 163 03991-03997M
1934		CD: Pearl GEMMCDS 9085

Der Tambour/Mörike-Lieder (Wenn meine Mutter hexen könnt')

Tokyo	Gurlitt	78: Victor (Japan) SD 3091
July 1952		LP: Victor (Japan) LS 2006

Treibe nur mit Lieben Spott/Spanisches Liederbuch

Berlin	Müller	HMV unpublished
October		
1934		

Berlin	Müller	HMV unpublished
November		
1934		

London	Müller	78: HMV DB 2703
February		LP: EMI RLS 759/1C 163 03991-03997M
1935		CD: Pearl GEMMCDS 9085

Und willst du deinen Liebsten sterben sehen/Italienisches Liederbuch

Berlin	Müller	78: HMV DB 2372
September		LP: Electrola E 83393
1934		LP: EMI RLS 759/1C 163 03991-03997M
		CD: Pearl GEMMCDS 9085

Wolf Lieder/concluded

Verborgenheit/Mörike-Lieder (Lass', o Welt, o lass' mich sein!)

Tokyo	Gurlitt	78: Victor (Japan) SD 3091
July 1952		LP: Victor (Japan) LS 2006

Wenn du mich mit den Augen streifst/Italienisches Liederbuch

Berlin	Müller	78: HMV DB 2372
September		LP: EMI RLS 759/1C 163 03991-03997M
1934		CD: Pearl GEMMCDS 9085

TRADITIONAL AND MISCELLANEOUS

Durch Oper und Operette: Grosses Electrola-Künstlertreffen

Berlin November 1935	Perras, Frind, Korjus, Jungkurth, Klose, Wittrisch, Strienz Orchestra and Chorus Seidler-Winkler	78: Electrola EH 945 78: HMV (Australia) EB 101 LP: OASI 556 <u>Hüsch is heard in short extracts from Aida, Rigoletto and Fledermaus</u>

Goldene Abendsonne

Berlin October 1930	Staatskapelle Weissmann	78: Parlophone/Odeon unpublished

Poggenkantate

Berlin June 1933	Instrumental accompaniment	Untraced radio broadcast <u>Hüsch also recites the text before the musical performance</u>

RECORDED INTERVIEWS

Speaks about oclecting his Lied repertoire

1938	LP: Toshiba EAC 77365-77368 CD: Toshiba Shinseido SRG 1004

Berlin Opera between the Wars

1938	LP: Toshiba EAC 77365-77368

Josef Metternich
born 1915

Discography compiled by John Hunt

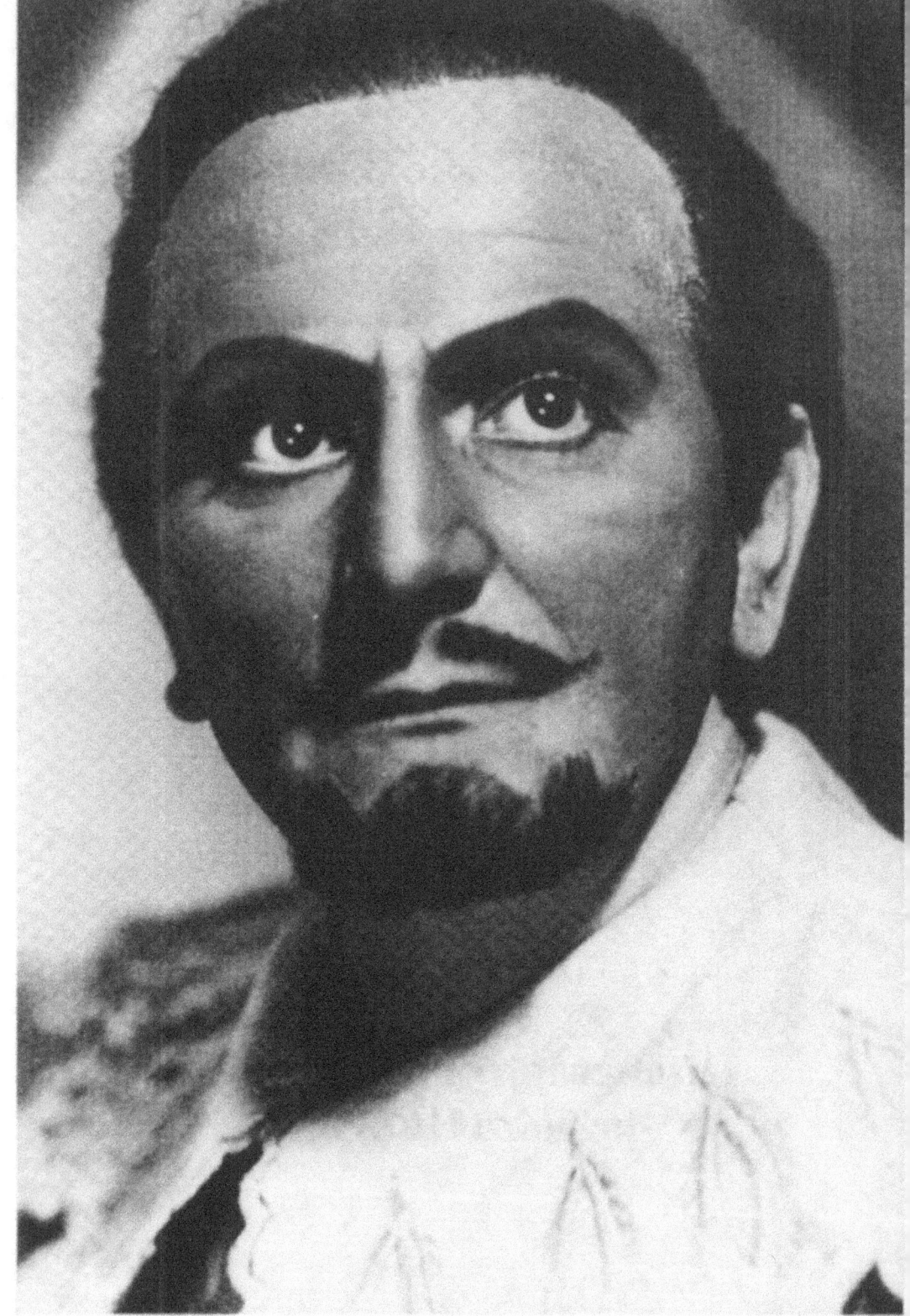

LUDWIG VAN BEETHOVEN (1770-1827)

Fidelio

Geneva November 1951	Role of Pizarro Werth, Otto, Anders, Weiser, Frick, Pantscheff Suisse Romande Orchestra & Chorus Fricsay	Unpublished radio broadcast
Vienna June 1953	Mödl, Schwarzkopf, Windgassen, Schock, Edelmann, Braun Wiener Singverein VSO Karajan	Unpublished radio broadcast

HAMBURGISCHE STAATSOPER
Intendant Dr. Günther Rennert

Sonnabend, den 15. September 1951, 19.30 Uhr
Sonnabend-Abonnement (2. Folge)

In neuer Inszenierung und Einstudierung

FIDELIO

Oper in zwei Aufzügen (4 Bildern)
von Ludwig van Beethoven
Musikalische Leitung: Leopold Ludwig
Inszenierung: Günther Rennert
Bühnenbild und Kostüm: Alfred Siercke
Chöre: Günter Hertel

Don Fernando, Minister	Mathieu Ahlersmeyer
Don Pizarro, Gouverneur eines Staatsgefängnisses	Josef Metternich
Florestan, ein Gefangener	Peter Anders
Leonore, seine Gemahlin, unter dem Namen „Fidelio"	Martha Mödl
Rocco, Kerkermeister	Theo Herrmann
Marzelline, seine Tochter	Lore Hoffmann
Jacquino, Pförtner	Kurt Marschner
Erster Gefangener	Fritz Göllnitz
Zweiter Gefangener..	Toni Blankenheim

Während der Verwandlung zum letzten Bild: 3. Leonoren-Ouvertüre

Im 4. Bild ist der Chor durch den Sonderchor der Hamburgischen Staatsoper verstärkt

Technische Leitung: Hermann Mendt und Karl Hahn

Pause nach dem 2. Bild

Beginn 19.30 Uhr   Ende 22.15 Uhr

HAMBURGISCHE STAATSOPER
Intendant Dr. Günther Rennert

Sonnabend, den 3. Oktober 1953, 19.30 Uhr
Sonnabend-Abonnement (1. Folge)

FIDELIO

Oper in zwei Aufzügen (4 Bildern)
von Ludwig van Beethoven

Musikalische Leitung: Leopold Ludwig
Inszenierung: Günther Rennert
Bühnenbild und Kostüm: Alfred Siercke
Chöre: Günter Hertel

Don Fernando, Minister	James Pease
Don Pizarro, Gouverneur eines Staatsgefängnisses	Josef Metternich
Florestan, ein Gefangener	Peter Anders
Leonore, seine Gemahlin, unter dem Namen „Fidelio"	Birgit Nilsson a. G.
Rocco, Kerkermeister	Theo Herrmann
Marzelline, seine Tochter	Lore Hoffmann
Jacquino, Pförtner	Kurt Marschner
Erster Gefangener	Fritz Göllnitz
Zweiter Gefangener	Toni Blankenheim

Während der Verwandlung zum letzten Bild: 3. Leonoren-Ouvertüre

Im 4. Bild ist der Chor durch den Sonderchor der Hamburgischen Staatsoper verstärkt

Technische Leitung: Hermann Mendt

Beginn 19.30 Uhr   Ende gegen 22.15 Uhr

GEORGES BIZET (1838-1875)

Carmen, excerpt (Votre toast!)

Berlin May 1953	Otto, Eustrati, Schaffrian Berlin SO Chorus Schüchter <u>Sung in German</u>	78: Electrola DB 11548 45: Electrola E 40087 LP: Electrola E 60059/E 80436/WBLP 502 　　VP 8009/SMVP 8009 LP: EMI 1C 047 50582/1C 137 769 1901 CD: EMI CDM 763 6742
Berlin January 1957	Berlin RO Fricsay <u>Sung in German</u>	LP: DG LPE 17 095 LP: Preiser PR 135013 CD: Preiser 90125
Munich January 1958	Bavarian State Orchestra & Chorus Fricsay <u>Sung in German</u>	LP: DG LPEM 19 153/LPEM 19 191/ 　　SLPEM 136 032/2535 297 CD: DG 447 8092

Carmen, excerpt (Su tu m'aimes, Carmen!)

Berlin May 1953	Berlin SO Chorus Schüchter <u>Sung in German</u>	45: Electrola E 50051 LP: Electrola E 60059/E 80436/WBLP 502 　　VP 8009/SMVP 8009

Les pêcheurs de perles, excerpt (Au fond du temple saint)

Berlin December 1957	Schock Berlin SO Schüchter <u>Sung in German</u>	45: Electrola E 40145 LP: Electrola E 60559/VP 8069/SMVP 8069 LP: EMI 1C 137 769 1901

ALEXANDER BORODIN (1833-1887)

Prince Igor, excerpt (No sleep, no rest)

Munich March 1957	Munich PO Sandberg <u>Sung in German</u>	45: DG EPL 30 300 LP: Preiser PR 135013 CD: Preiser 90125

GAETONO DONIZETTI (1797-1848)

Lucia di Lammermoor

Munich December 1956	<u>Role of Enrico</u> Köth, Töpper, Simandy, Holm, Klarwein, Engen Bavarian State Orchestra & Chorus Fricsay <u>Sung in German</u>	Unpublished radio broadcast <u>Tapes partially destroyed</u>

Lucia di Lammermoor, excerpt (Egli s'avanza!)

Berlin January 1957	Köth Berlin SO Schüchter <u>Sung in German</u>	45: Electrola E 50066 LP: Electrola E 80021 LP: EMI 1C 047 28579/1C 047 28598/ 1C 137 769 1901

Lucia di Lammermoor, (Chi mi frema)

Berlin January 1957	Köth, Töpper, Schock, Frick, Schmidt Berlin SO Städtische Oper Chorus Schüchter <u>Sung in German</u>	45: Electrola E 50066 LP: Electrola E 60074/E 80021/WBLP 530 LP: EMI 1C 047 28579

UMBERTO GIORDANO (1867-1948)

Andrea Chenier

Munich 1954	Role of Gérard Schech, Benningsen, Hopf, Berry Bavarian Radio Orchestra & Chorus Sawallisch Sung in German	Unpublished radio broadcast

Andrea Chenier, excerpt (Nemico della patria?)

Munich January 1959	Bamberg SO Prohaska Sung in German	45: DG EPL 30 425 LP: Preiser PR 135013 CD: Preiser 90125

CHARLES GOUNOD (1818-1893)

Faust, excerpt (Avant de quitter ces lieux)

Berlin April 1953	Berlin SO Schüchter Sung in German	78: Electrola DB 11547 45: Electrola E 30076/E 50087 LP: EMI 1C 047 28598/1C 137 769 1901

ENGELBERT HUMPERDINCK (1854-1921)

Hänsel und Gretel

London June- July 1953	Role of Peter Schwarzkopf, Grümmer, Ilosvay,Schürhoff, Felbermayer Philharmonia Choruses Karajan	LP: Columbia 33CX 1096-1097 LP: Columbia (Germany) C 90327-90328 LP: Angel 3506 LP: World Records OC 187-188 LP: EMI SLS 5145 CD: EMI CMS 769 2932 Excerpts LP: Columbia 33CX 1819 LP: Columbia (Germany) C 80528 LP: World Records OH 189

EMMERICH KALMAN (1882-1953)

Der Zigeunerprimas

Cologne 1949	Role of Racz Katona, Losch, W.Hofmann WDR Orchestra and Chorus Marszalek	Unpublished radio broadcast

WALTER KOLLO (1878-1940)

Derfflinger, excerpt (Heimat, du Inbegriff der Liebe)

Berlin April 1957	Berlin SO Schüchter	45: Electrola 7EG 8708/E 40131 LP: Electrola VP 8070/SMVP 8070 LP: EMI 1C 137 769 1901 CD: EMI CDM 763 6742

RUGGIERO LEONCAVALLO (1858-1918)

I pagliacci

Berlin
June 1959
	Role of Tonio
	Muszely, Schock,
	Cordes, Schmidt
	Staatskapelle
	and Chorus
	Stein
	Sung in German
		LP: Electrola E 80501-80502/
		   STE 80501-80502
		Excerpts
		LP: Electrola E 80617/SME 80617/
		   1C 063 28999

I pagliacci, excerpt (Si può?)

Berlin May 1953	Berlin SO Schüchter Sung in German	78: Electrola DB 11548 45: Electrola E 30075/E 40088 LP: Electrola E 60079/VP 8069/SMVP 8069 VP 8012/SMVP 8012 LP: EMI 1C 047 28571/1C 137 769 1901 CD: EMI CDM 763 6742

PAUL LINCKE (1866-1946)

Frau Luna, excerpt (Isola bella)

Berlin April 1957	Berlin SO Arndt Choir Schüchter	45: Electrola 7EG 8708/E 40131 LP: Electrola VP 8070/SMVP 8070 LP: EMI 1C 137 769 1901 CD: EMI CDM 763 6742

Im Reich der Indra, excerpt (Es war einmal)

Berlin August 1953	Berlin SO Schüchter	45: Electrola 7EG 7990/E 20003 LP: EMI 1C 137 769 1901 CD: EMI CDM 763 6742

GUSTAV MAHLER (1860-1911)

Lieder eines fahrenden Gesellen

1950	Orchestra L.Ludwig	LP: Urania URLP 7016

HEINRICH MARSCHNER (1795-1861)

Hans Heiling, excerpt (An jenem Tag)

Berlin February 1956	Berlin RO L.Ludwig	45: DG EPL 30 249 LP: DG LPE 17 095 LP: Preiser PR 135013 CD: Preiser 90125

BAYERISCHE STAATSOPER

MÜNCHNER FESTSPIELE

RICHARD STRAUSS
Händel – Mozart – Wagner – Pfitzner

MÜNCHNER OPERNFESTSPIELE

München, Freitag, 19. August 1955

Die Frau ohne Schatten

Oper in 3 Akten von Hugo von Hofmannsthal
Musik von **RICHARD STRAUSS**

Musikalische Leitung: George Sebastian — Inszenierung: Rudolf Hartmann
Bühnenbild und Kostüme: Emil Preetorius

Der Kaiser	Hans Hopf
Die Kaiserin	Leonie Rysanek
Die Amme	Lilian Benningsen
Der Geisterbote	Kurt Böhme
Hüter der Schwelle	Erika Köth
Erscheinung eines Jünglings	Howard Vandenburg
Stimme des Falken	Gerda Sommerschuh
Stimme von oben	Ina Gerhein
Barak, der Färber	Josef Metternich
Sein Weib	Marianne Schech
Der Einäugige ⎫	Karl Hoppe
Der Einarmige ⎬ des Färbers Brüder	Rudolf Wünzer
Der Bucklige ⎭	Karl Ostertag
Stimmen der Ungeborenen	Erika Köth
	Anny van Kruyswyk
	Antonie Fahberg
	Elisabeth Lindermeier
	Ruth Michaelis
	Ina Gerhein
Erster Wächter	Max Proebstl
Zweiter Wächter	Karl Hoppe
Dritter Wächter	Hans Hermann Nissen
Erste Dienerin	Erika Köth
Zweite Dienerin	Antonie Fahberg
Dritte Dienerin	Ruth Michaelis

Kaiserliche Diener. Fremde Kinder. Geisterstimmen

Ort der Handlung:
1. Akt: Auf einer Terrasse über den kaiserlichen Gärten. Färberhaus.
2. Akt: Färberhaus. Wald v. d. Pavillon des Falkners. Färberhaus. Schlafgemach d. Kaiserin. Färberhaus
3. Akt: Unterirdischer Kerker. Geistertempel: Eingang. Geistertempel: Inneres. Landschaft im Geisterreich

Solo-Violine: Herbert Becker — Solo-Cello: Oswald Uhl

Technische Oberleitung: Emil Buchenberger - Chöre: Herbert Erlenwein
Anfertigung der Kostüme: Alexander Stenz-Hentze - Maskenbildner: Georg Rasche
Anfertigung der Dekorationen: Ludwig Hornsteiner - Technische Einrichtung: Anton Ott
Beleuchtung: Josef Dusch und Ludwig Bourdillon
Inspektion: Anton Hackel und Martin Brucklachner - Souffleur: Hans Vogt

Anfang 18 Uhr   Pausen nach dem 1. und 2. Akt   Ende gegen 22½ Uhr

Erfrischungsraum gegenüber der Eintrittskartenkasse

PIETRO MASCAGNI (1863-1945)

Cavalleria rusticana, excerpt (Il Signore vi manda, compar Alfio!)

Berlin	Rysanek	LP: Electrola E 60076/WBLP 534/
October 1955	Deutsche Oper	E 80617/SME 80617
	Orchestra	LP: EMI 1C 063 28999/1C147 29150-29151M/
	Schüchter	1C 137 769 1901
	Sung in German	CD: EMI CDM 763 6742

Cavalleria rusticana, excerpt (Il cavallo scalpita)

Berlin	Deutsche Oper	LP: Electrola E 60076/WBLP 534/E 70011/
October 1955	Orchestra & Chorus	E 80617/SME 80617
	Schüchter	LP: EMI 1C 063 28999/1C 137 769 1901
	Sung in German	

GIACOMO MEYERBEER (1791-1864)

L'Africaine, excerpt (Fille des rois!)

Munich October 1954	Bavarian RO Lehmann Sung in German	78: DG LM 62 934 45: DG NL 32 024 LP: DG LPE 17 095 LP: Preiser PR 135013 CD: Preiser 90125

L'Africaine, excerpt (Adamastor, roi des vagues!)

Berlin April 1958	Berlin SO Chorus Schüchter Sung in German	45: Electrola E 30416 LP: EMI 1C 047 28598/1C 137 769 1901

CARL MILLOECKER (1842-1899)

Gasparone

Cologne 1956	Role of Stranger Schlemm, Talmar, Kusche, Gehly WDR Orchestra and Chorus Marszalek	Unpublished radio broadcast Excerpt LP: RCA VL 30353

Gasparone, excerpt (Dunkelrote Rosen)

Berlin August 1953	Berlin SO Schüchter	45: Electrola 7EG 7990/E 40131/E 20003 LP: Electrola VP 8070/SMVP 8070 LP: EMI 1C 137 769 1901 CD: EMI CDM 763 6742

WOLFGANG AMADEUS MOZART (1756-1791)

Don Giovanni, excerpt (La ci darem la mano)

Berlin	Schlemm	45: DG EPL 30 274
November 1956	Berlin RO	LP: Preiser PR 135013
	Rennert	CD: Preiser 90125
	Sung in German	

Le nozze di Figaro, excerpt (Hai già vinto la causa!)

Berlin	Berlin RO	45: DG EPL 30 249
February 1956	L.Ludwig	LP: DG LPE 17 095/LPEM 19 066
	Sung in German	LP: Preiser PR 135013
		CD: Preiser 90125

Le nozze di Figaro, excerpt (Non più andrai)

Berlin	Berlin SO	78: Electrola DA 5522
February 1954	Schüchter	45: Electrola E 50087
	Sung in German	LP: EMI SHZE 121/1C 137 769 1901

Le nozze di Figaro, excerpt (Aprite un po' quegl' occhi!)

Berlin	Berlin SO	78: Electrola DA 5522
February 1954	Schüchter	45: Electrola E 50087
	Sung in German	LP: EMI 1C 047 28598/1C 137 769 1901
		CD: EMI CDM 763 6742

JACQUES OFFENBACH (1819-1880)

Les contes d'Hoffmann, excerpt (Scintille diamant!)

Berlin	Berlin SO	78: Electrola DB 11564
February 1954	Schüchter	45: Electrola E 30095/E 40087/E 50052
	<u>Sung in German</u>	LP: Electrola E 60061
		LP: EMI 1C 047 28577/1C 047 28598/
		1C 137 769 1901
		CD: EMI CDM 763 6742

Les contes d'Hoffmann, excerpt (Tu ne chanteras plus?)

Berlin	Streich, Klose	45: Electrola E 50088
November 1954	Berlin SO	LP: Electrola E 60061
	Schüchter	LP: EMI 1C 047 28181/1C 047 28577
	<u>Sung in German</u>	

AMILCARE PONCHIELLI (1834-1886)

La Gioconda, excerpt (Maledici?/O monumento!)

Munich	Bamberg SO	45: DG EPL 30 425
January 1959	Prohaska	LP: Preiser PR 135013
	<u>Sung in German</u>	CD: Preiser 90125

GIACOMO PUCCINI (1858-1924)

Il tabarro, excerpt (Scorri fiume eterno!)

Munich	Bamberg SO	45: DG EPL 30 425
January 1959	Prohaska	LP: Preiser PR 135013
	<u>Sung in German</u>	CD: Preiser 90125

132 Metternich

Tosca

Hamburg April 1953	Role of Scarpia Martinis, Schock, Kusche NDR Orchestra and Chorus Schüchter Sung in German	LP: Ed Smith EJS 508 LP: Eurodisc 300.727 420 Incorrectly described by Ed Smith as a Berlin 1946 performance with Welitsch and Rosvaenge, conducted by Moralt
Munich 1953	Rysanek, Hopf, Faulhaber Bavarian Radio Orchestra & Chorus Kraus Sung in German	LP: Melodram MEL 436

Tosca, excerpt (Tre sbirri)

Berlin October 1955	H.Kraus Deutsche Oper Orchestra & Chorus Schüchter Sung in German	78: Electrola DB 11592 45: Electrola E 40086 LP: Electrola E 70011 LP: EMI 1C 137 769 1901
Berlin September 1959	Zimmermann Berlin SO Deutsche Oper Chorus Klobucar Sung in German	LP: Electrola E 70079/E 80538/ SME 80538/CSDW 7024 LP: EMI 1C 063 28509 CD: EMI CDZ 252 3482

Tosca, excerpt (Già mi dicon venal)

Berlin April 1958	Berlin SO Schüchter Sung in German	45: Electrola E 30416 LP: EMI 1C 047 28598/1C 137 769 1901 CD: EMI CDM 763 6742
Berlin September 1959	Berlin SO Klobucar Sung in German	LP: Electrola E 80538/SME 80538/CSDW 7024 LP: EMI 1C 063 28509 CD: EMI CZS 252 3482

GIOACHINO ROSSINI (1792-1868)

Il barbiere di Siviglia, excerpt (Largo al factotum)

Berlin April 1953	Berlin SO Schüchter Sung in German	78: Electrola DB 11547 45: Electrola E 30076/E 50087 LP: Electrola VP 8069/SMVP 8069 LP: EMI 1C 137 769 1901 CD: EMI CDM 763 6742
Berlin January 1957	Berlin RO Fricsay Sung in German	LP: DG LPE 17 095/88 025 LP: Preiser PR 135013 CD: Preiser 90125

RICHARD STRAUSS (1864-1949)

Arabella

Berlin December 1950	Role of Mandryka Goltz, Schlemm, Witte, Pflanzl Staatskapelle and Chorus Keilberth	Unpublished radio broadcast

Arabella, scenes: 1.Welko das Bild!; 2.Sie wollen mich heiraten?/Und du sollst mein Gebieter sein; 3.Und jetzt sag' ich ihm Adieu; 4.Das war sehr gut, Mandryka

London
September-
October 1954
	Schwarzkopf,
	Felbermayer,
	Gedda, Schlott
	Philharmonia
	Matacic
		45: Columbia SEL 1579 (4)
		45: Columbia (Germany) C 30166
		LP: Columbia 33CX 1226/33CX 1897
		LP: Columbia (Germany) C 80619/C 90406
		LP: Angel 35094
		LP: World Records OH 199
		LP: EMI RLS 154 6133 (2,3,4)/RLS 751/
		    1C 037 03297M
		CD: EMI CDH 761 0012 (2,3,4)/
		    CDM 565 5772 (4)

Die Frau ohne Schatten

Munich August 1954	Role of Barak Rysanek, Schech, Benningsen, Hopf, Böhme Bavarian State Orchestra & Chorus Kempe	LP: Melodram MEL 108 CD: Voce della luna VL 20073

Salome

Vienna 1952	Role of Jochanaan Wegner, Milinkovic, Szemere, Kmennt VSO Moralt	LP: Philips ABL 3003-3004/A00163-00164L/ 6747 406 LP: Columbia (USA) SL 126 CD: Philips 438 6642

PIOTR TCHAIKOVSKY (1840–1893)

Evgeny Onegin, excerpt (You have written to me)

Munich October 1954	Bavarian RO Lehmann <u>Sung in German</u>	78: DG LM 62 934 45: DG NL 32 024 LP: DG LPE 17 095/LPEM 19 023 LP: Preiser PR 135013 CD: Preiser 90125

Pique Dame, excerpt (I love you beyond all measure)

Munich February 1957	Schlemm Munich PO Sandberg <u>Sung in German</u>	45: DG EPL 30 300 LP: Preiser PR 135013 CD: Preiser 90125

GIUSEPPE VERDI (1813-1901)

Aida

Hamburg 1951	Role of Amonasro Zadek, Höngen, Rosvaenge NDR Orchestra and Chorus Schmidt-Isserstedt Sung in German	LP: Cetra LO

Aida, excerpt (Ciel! Mio padre!/Ma dimmi, per qual via?)

Berlin October 1955	Rysanek, Wagner, Schock, Roth-Ehrang Berlin SO Schüchter Sung in German	LP: Electrola E 70003/E 80588 LP: EMI 1C 047 28581/1C147 29150-29151

Un ballo in maschera

New York January 1955	Role of Renato Milanov, Peters, Madeira, Tucker Metropolitan Opera Orchestra & Chorus Mitropoulos	LP: Raritas OPR 408 LP: Cetra LO 4 LP: Foyer FO 1020 CD: Foyer 2CF-2004 Excerpts LP: Gioielli della lirica GML 13
Munich 1956	Nilsson, Köth, Madeira, Feiersinger Bavarian State Orchestra & Chorus Erede Sung in German	Unpublished radio broadcast
Munich December 1957	Cunitz, Steffek, Benningsen, Simandy Bavarian State Orchestra & Chorus Fricsay Sung in German	Unpublished radio broadcast

DEUTSCHE STAATSOPER

Montag, den 8. März 1954

OTHELLO
Oper in vier Akten von Arrigo Boito

Musik von Giuseppe Verdi

Musikalische Leitung: Wilhelm Loibner
Inszenierung: Michael Bohnen · Chöre: Karl Schmidt
Bühnenbild: Hainer Hill · Kostüme: Gisela Appelt

Othello, Mohr, Befehlshaber der venezianischen Flotte	Peter Anders a. G.
Jago, Fähnrich	Joseph Metternich a. G.
Cassio, Hauptmann	Gerhard Stolze
Rodrigo, ein edler Venezianer	Alwin Hendriks
Lodovico, Gesandter der Republik Venedig	Gustav Köysti
Montano, der Vorgänger Othellos in der Statthalterei von Cypern	Walter Großmann
Ein Herold	Horst Jakob
Desdemona, Othellos Gemahlin	Helma Prechter a. G.
Emilia, Jagos Gattin	Adelheid Müller-Heß

Soldaten, Seeleute, Edeldamen und venezianische Nobile, Krieger, Volk

Ort: Eine Hafenstadt der Insel Cypern
Zeit: Ende des 15. Jahrhunderts

Technische Leitung: Max Hübner
Regie-Assistenz: Udo Esselun
Inspizient: Horst Wruck

Kleine Pause nach dem 1. Akt — Große Pause nach dem 2. Akt

DEUTSCHE STAATSOPER
ADMIRALSPALAST · FRIEDRICHSTRASSE 101–102

Mittwoch, den 25. Dezember 1946

La Traviata
(VIOLETTA)

Oper in 3 Akten (4 Bildern)

Text nach dem Dumas'schen Schauspiel „Die Dame mit den Camelien" von F. M. Piave

Musik von Giuseppe Verdi

Musikalische Leitung	Karl Schmidt
Inszenierung	Wolf Völker

Violetta Valery	Erna Berger
Flora Bervoix	Hilde Dullin
Annina, Violetta's Dienerin	Elisabeth Aldor
Alfred Germont	Peter Anders
Georg Germont, sein Vater	Josef Metternich a. G.
Gaston, Vicomte von Letorières	Paul Schmidtmann
Baron Douphol	Walter Großmann
Marquis d'Obigny	Willi Pollow
Doktor Grenvil	Otto Hopf
Josef, Violetta's Diener	Gerhard Witting
Eine Zigeunerin	Elfriede Marherr
Ein Kommissionär	Kay Willumsen
Zwei Gäste	Ernst Schall, Otto Wünsche

Freunde von Violetta und Flora, Landleute

1. Bild: Tarantella getanzt von Ilse Schulz, Harald Mariste, Herbert Hanschke
3. Bild: Stierkämpfer: Willi Altvater

Tänzerinnen: Sigrid Logan, Börge Vermeer, Lisa Althaus, Edith Gohlke, Hiltraud Henning, Gisela Vesco, Vera van Dooren, Josefa Fial

Ort der Handlung: Paris und seine Umgebung um 1860

1. Bild: Nächtlicher Garten bei Violetta
2. Bild: Landhaus in der Nähe von Paris
3. Bild: Maskenball bei Flora
4. Bild: Schlafzimmer Violettas

Gesamtausstattung	Paul Strecker
Chöre	Karl Reibe
Technische Leitung	Max Hübner

Pause nach dem 2. Bild

Un ballo in maschera, excerpt (Alla vita che t'arride)

Berlin	Berlin SO	78: Electrola DB 11558
August 1953	Schüchter	LP: EMI 1C 137 769 1901
	Sung in German	CD: EMI CDM 763 6742

Un ballo in maschera, excerpt (Alzati!/Eri tu)

Berlin	Berlin SO	78: Electrola DB 11558
August 1953	Schüchter	45: Electrola E 50065
	Sung in German	LP: Electrola E 70011
		LP: EMI 1C 047 28598/1C 137 769 1901
		CD: EMI CDM 763 6742

Don Carlo, excerpt (E lui desso! L'Infante!)

Berlin	Schock	78: Electrola DB 11572
December 1954	Berlin SO	45: Electrola E 30091/E 40083
	Schüchter	LP: Electrola E 60559/WCLP 516/
	Sung in German	VP 8069/SMVP 8069
		CD: EMI CDM 763 6742/CZS 767 1832

Falstaff

Munich	Role of Falstaff	Unpublished radio broadcast
1952-1954	Watson, Töpper,	
	Ostertag,	
	Fischer-Dieskau	
	Bavarian State	
	Orchestra & Chorus	
	Zallinger	
	Sung in German	

Falstaff, excerpt (Va, vecchio John!)

Berlin	Fischer-Dieskau	45: DG 36 016
January 1951	Berlin RO	LP: DG LPEM 19 029
	Fricsay	CD: Preiser 90125
	Sung in German	

La forza del destino

Hamburg 1952	Role of Carlo Martinis, Mödl, Schock, Frick, Neidlinger NDR Orchestra and Chorus Schmidt-Isserstedt Sung in German	LP: Eurodisc 300.724 435

La forza del destino, excerpt (Invano Alvaro tu celasti al mondo)

Berlin May 1955	Schock Berlin SO Schüchter Sung in German	LP: Electrola E 60559/WCLP 516/ VP 8069/SMVP 8069 LP: EMI 1C 137 769 1901

La forza del destino, excerpt (Solenne in quest' ora)

Berlin December 1954	Schock Berlin SO Schüchter Sung in German	78: Electrola DB 11572 45: Electrola E 40083 LP: Electrola E 60559/WCLP 516/ VP 8069/SMVP 8069 LP: EMI 1C 137 769 1901

La forza del destino, excerpt (Son Pereda, son ricco d'onore)

Berlin November 1954	Berlin SO Grüber Sung in German	78: Electrola DB 11579 45: Electrola E 50073 LP: Electrola E 70011 LP: EMI 1C 137 769 1901

La forza del destino, excerpt (Urna fatale del mio destino)

Berlin November 1954	Berlin SO Grüber Sung in German	78: Electrola DB 11579 LP: Electrola E 70011 LP: EMI 1C 047 28598/1C 137 769 1901

Macbeth

~~Dresden~~ *Berlin*
September 1950
Role of Macbeth
Mödl, Hülgert,
T.Hermann
Staatskapelle
and Chorus
Keilberth
Sung in German

Unpublished radio broadcast

Cologne
September 1954
Varnay, Geisler,
Weber
WDR Orchestra
and Chorus
Kraus
Sung in German

CD: Myto MCD 952128

Otello

Berlin
January 1951
Role of Iago
Trötschel, Anders
Berlin Radio
Orchestra & Chorus
Fricsay
Sung in German

Unpublished radio broadcast
Only parts of the recording may
be preserved

Munich
May 1956
Kupper, Hopf
Bavarian State
Orchestra & Chorus
Fricsay
Sung in German

Unpublished radio broadcast

Cologne
1958
Watson, Hopf
WDR Orchestra
and Chorus
Solti
Sung in German

Unpublished radio broadcast

Munich
March 1960
Watson, Uhl
Bavarian State
Orchestra & Chorus
Fricsay
Sung in German

Unpublished radio broadcast

Otello, excerpt (Credo in un dio crudel!)

Berlin October 1955	Deutsche Oper Orchestra Schüchter <u>Sung in German</u>	78: Electrola DB 11592 45: Electrola E 40086 LP: Electrola E 70011 LP: EMI 1C 047 28598/1C 137 769 1901 CD: EMI CDM 763 6742

Otello, excerpt (Era la notte)

Berlin December 1957	Schock Berlin SO Schüchter <u>Sung in German</u>	45: Electrola E 40145 LP: Electrola E 60559/WCLP 516/ VP 8069/SMVP 8069 LP: EMI 1C 137 769 1901

Rigoletto

Berlin September 1950	<u>Role of Rigoletto</u> Streich, Klose, Schock Berlin Radio Orchestra & Chorus Fricsay <u>Sung in German</u>	CD: Myto MCD 94511
Cologne 1956	Coertse, De Luca, Frick WDR Orchestra and Chorus Rossi <u>Sung in German</u>	Unpublished radio broadcast

HAMBURGISCHE STAATSOPER
Intendant Heinz Tietjen

Donnerstag, den 11. Juni 1959
Donnerstag-Abonnement (1. Folge)

In der Neuinszenierung

DIE MACHT DES SCHICKSALS

Oper in drei Akten (acht Bildern) von Giuseppe Verdi
Text von Francesco Maria Piave, deutsche Fassung von Georg Göhler

Musikalische Leitung: Leopold Ludwig
Inszenierung: Ernst Poettgen
Ausstattung: Heinz Pfeiffenberger
Chöre: Günter Hertel

Der Marchese von Calatrava	Sigmund Roth
Leonore di Vargas, seine Tochter	Clara Ebers
Don Carlos di Vargas, sein Sohn	Josef Metternich
Alvaro	Kurt Ruesche
Preziosilla, eine Zigeunerin	Cvetka Ahlin-Soucek
Pater Guardian	Arnold van Mill
Fra Melitone	Theo Herrmann
Curra, Leonores Zofe	Hildegard Rütgers
Alcalde	Karl Otto
Mastro Trabuco, Maultiertreiber	Jürgen Förster
Ein Chirurgus im spanischen Heer	Jean Pfendt

Im zweiten Bild tanzen: Christel Teelen, Marion Briner, Inge Jäger
Im sechsten Bild: Joachim Weinberg und die Damen und Herren des Balletts

Es spielt das Philharmonische Staatsorchester

Technische Leitung: Hermann Mendt - Bühnentechnische Einrichtung: Hans Stahn
Kostümausführung: Anneliese Meier - Chefmaskenbildner: Max Vojta
Beleuchtung: Günther Metzeld - Inspektion: Guido Diemer, Jürgen Weise

Pause nach dem vierten Bild

Beginn 19.30 Uhr   Ende gegen 22.45 Uhr

HAMBURGISCHE STAATSOPER
Intendant Dr. Günther Rennert

Mittwoch, den 28. April 1954, 19.30 Uhr
Mittwoch-Abonnement (1. Folge)

AROLDO

Oper in vier Akten von F. M. Piave
Musik von Giuseppe Verdi
in der Bearbeitung der Hamburgischen Staatsoper
unter Verwendung der Übersetzung von A. Leschetizky

Musikalische Leitung: Hans Georg Ratjen a. G.
Inszenierung: Günther Rennert
Bühnenbild u. Kostüm: Dominik Hartmann a. G.
Chöre: Günter Hertel

Aroldo, ein Kreuzfahrer	Peter Anders
Nina, seine Gattin	Anne Bollinger
Egberto, deren Vater, Vasall des Herzogs von Kent	Josef Metternich
Briano, ein Kreuzfahrer und Kampfgefährte Aroldos	James Pease
Godvino } Gäste im Hause Egbertos	Fritz Lehnert
Enrico	Hermann Prey

Edelleute, Schottische Landleute, Fischer

Erster und dritter Akt: Im Schlosse Egbertos
Zweiter Akt: Friedhof
Vierter Akt: Küste Schottlands

Zeit: Um 1200

Technische Leitung: Hermann Mendt

Pause nach dem 2. Akt (2. Bild)

Rigoletto, excerpt (Cortigiani, vil razza dannata!)

Berlin	Berlin SO	78: Electrola DB 11549
June 1953	Schüchter	45: Electrola E 30074/E 50073
	<u>Sung in German</u>	LP: Electrola E 60060/E 80436
		LP: EMI 1C 047 28567/1C 047 28598/
		1C 137 769 1901/VP 8006/SMVP 8006
		CD: EMI CDM 763 6742

Rigoletto, excerpt (Bella figlia dell' amore)

Berlin	Köth, Wagner,	78: Electrola DB 11565
June 1953	Schock, Frick	45: Electrola E 50065
	Berlin SO	LP: Electrola E 60060/E 80436
	Schüchter	LP: EMI 1C 047 28567/1C 137 769 1901
	<u>Sung in German</u>	VP 8006/SMVP 8006

Rigoletto, excerpt (Egli è là! Morto!)

Berlin	Köth	LP: Electrola E 60060
June 1953	Berlin SO	LP: EMI 1C 047 28567
	Schüchter	
	<u>Sung in German</u>	

La traviata

Frankfurt 1952	Ebers, Holm Hessischer Rundfunk Orchestra and Chorus Molinari-Pradelli Sung in German	Unpublished radio broadcast

La traviata, Act 3

Berlin January 1951	Trötschel, Anders Berlin Radio Orchestra & Chorus Fricsay Sung in German	Unpublished radio broadcast

La traviata, excerpt (Di provenza il mar)

Berlin June 1953	Berlin SO Schüchter Sung in German	78: Electrola DB 11549 45: Electrola E 30074/E 40088 LP: Electrola E 60046/E 60071/ E 80037/STE 80037 LP: EMI 1C 047 28598/1C 137 769 1901

La traviata, excerpt (Invitato a qui seguirmi)

Berlin June 1953	Muszely, Müller, Schock, Schmidt, Stoll, Kohn Berlin SO and Chorus Schüchter Sung in German	LP: Electrola E 60046/E 80037/STE 80037

La traviata, excerpt (Madamigella Valéry?)

Berlin February 1959	Muszely Staatskapelle Berlin SO Sung in German	LP: Electrola E 60651

HAMBURGISCHE STAATSOPER
Intendant Dr. Günther Rennert

Freitag, den 17. Februar 1956, 19.30 Uhr
Freitag-Abonnement (2. Folge)

DER FLIEGENDE HOLLÄNDER

Romantische Oper in drei Akten von Richard Wagner

Musikalische Leitung: Leopold Ludwig
Inszenierung: Georg Hartmann
Bühnenbild und Kostüm: Dominik Hartmann
Chöre: Günter Hertel

Daland, ein norwegischer Seefahrer	Arnold van Mill
Senta, seine Tochter	Helene Werth
Erik, der Jäger	Walter Geisler
Mary, Sentas Amme	Gusta Hammer
Der Steuermann Dalands	Fritz Lehnert
Der Holländer	Josef Metternich

Matrosen des Norwegers – Die Mannschaft des Fliegenden Holländers –
Szene: Die norwegische Küste

Im 3. Akt wird der Chor der Hamburgischen Staats
durch den Herren-Sonderchor verstärkt.

Pause nach dem 2. Akt

Technische Leitung: Hermann Menu.

BAYERISCHE STAATSOPER
NATIONALTHEATER MÜNCHEN

ZUM 100JÄHRIGEN JUBILÄUM DER URAUFFÜHRUNG
IM NATIONALTHEATER MÜNCHEN

Freitag, 21. Juni 1968

Die Meistersinger von Nürnberg

in drei Aufzügen von

RICHARD WAGNER

Musikalische Leitung: Joseph Keilberth · Inszenierung: Rudolf Hartmann
Bühnenbild: Helmut Jürgens · Kostüme: Sophia Schröck

PERSONEN

Hans Sachs, Schuster		Otto Wiener
Veit Pogner, Goldschmied		Gottlob Frick
Kunz Vogelgesang, Kürschner		Georg Paskuda
Konrad Nachtigall, Spengler		Raimund Grumbach
Sixtus Beckmesser, Stadtschreiber		Benno Kusche
Fritz Kothner, Bäcker	Meister-	Josef Metternich
Balthasar Zorn, Zinngießer	singer	Walther Carnuth
Ulrich Eißlinger, Würzkrämer		Franz Klarwein
Augustin Moser, Schneider		Karl Ostertag
Hermann Ortel, Seifensieder		Adolf Keil
Hans Schwarz, Strumpfwirker		Günter Missenhardt
Hans Folz, Kupferschmied		Max Proebstl
Walther von Stolzing, ein Ritter aus Franken		Ernst Kozub
David, Sachsen's Lehrbube		Friedrich Lenz
Eva, Pogners Tochter		Leonore Kirschstein
Magdalena, Eva's Amme		Hertha Töpper
Ein Nachtwächter		Hans Bruno Ernst

Bürger und Frauen aller Zünfte, Gesellen, Lehrbuben, Mädchen, Volk
Nürnberg, um die Mitte des 16. Jahrhunderts

Gesamtchor der Bayerischen Staatsoper
verstärkt durch den Aushilfs-Chor und Mitglieder des Lehrergesangvereins
Einstudierung: Wolfgang Baumgart

Il trovatore

Cologne May 1953	Role of Luna Goltz, Malaniuk, Hopf, Schirp WDR Orchestra and Chorus Fricsay Sung in German	Unpublished radio broadcast

Il trovatore, excerpt (Il balen del suo sorriso)

Berlin May 1954	Lang Berlin SO Deutsche Oper Chorus Schüchter Sung in German	78: Electrola DB 11568 45: Electrola E 50055 LP: Electrola E 60618/WDLP 642/ VP 8069/SMVP 8069 LP: EMI 1C 047 28998/1C 137 769 1901 CD: EMI CDM 763 6742

Il trovatore, excerpt (Tace la notte/Deserto sulla terra/Di geloso amor sprezzato)

Berlin February 1959	Muszely, Schock Berlin SO Zanotelli Sung in German	LP: Electrola E 80462/STE 80462 CD: EMI CDZ 252 2182/CZS 253 0472

Il trovatore, excerpt (Udiste? Come albeggi/Vivra! Contende il giubilio!)

Berlin February 1959	Muszely Berlin SO Zanotelli Sung in German	LP: Electrola E 80462/E 60618/E 60651/ WDLP 642/STE 80462 LP: EMI 1C 063 28998/1C 047 28598 CD: EMI CDZ 252 2182/CZS 253 0472 1C 047 28598 states, probably incorrectly, that this is a 1958 recording conducted by Schüchter

Il trovatore, excerpt (Ai nostri monti...to end of opera)

Berlin February 1959	Muszely, Wagner, Schock Berlin SO Zanotelli Sung in German	LP: Electrola E 60618/WDLP 642/ E 80462/STE 80462 LP: EMI 1C 063 28998 CD: EMI CDZ 252 2182/CZS 253 0472

RICHARD WAGNER (1813-1883)

Der fliegende Holländer

Berlin
October 1952
	Role of Holländer
	Kupper, Wagner,
	Windgassen,
	Haefliger, Greindl
	Berlin Radio
	Orchestra & Chorus
	Fricsay
		LP: DG LPM 18 116-18 118/
		  LPM 18 063-18 065/2701 009
		CD: DG 439 7142
		Excerpts
		45: DG NL 30 098/NL 32 098/
		  EPL 30 142/EPL 30 446
		LP: DG LPE 17 022/LPEM 19 122

Lohengrin

Hamburg July 1953	Role of Telramund Cunitz, Klose, Schock, Günther, Frick NDR Orchestra and Chorus Schüchter	LP: HMV ALP 1095-1098 LP: Electrola E 90061-90064 LP: Victor LHMV 1095-1098 CD: EMI CHS 565 5172 Excerpts LP: EMI 1C 047 01955M/1C 047 28598 CD: EMI CDM 763 6742

Die Meistersinger von Nürnberg

Munich November 1963	Role of Kothner Watson, Benningsen, Thomas, Lenz, Wiener, Kusche, Hotter Bavarian State Orchestra & Chorus Keilberth	LP: Eurodisc XR 70851 CD: Eurodisc GD 69008 Re-opening performance in Munich Nationaltheater

Das Rheingold

Hamburg 1952	Role of Donner L.Hoffman, R.Fischer, Windgassen, Schock, Greindl, Frick NDR Orchestra Schüchter	Unpublished radio broadcast

150 Metternich

Das Rheingold, scenes 1 and 4

Berlin	Blatter, Schock,	LP: HMV ALP 1984/ASD 535
March 1959	Melchert, Frantz	LP: Electrola E 80470/STE 80470/CSDW 7010
	Staatskapelle	LP: Eterna 825.091
	Kempe	LP: EMI CFP 109
		CD: EMI CMS 565 2122
		CD: Berlin Classics BC 20035

Tristan und Isolde

New York	Role of Kurwenal	Unpublished Met broadcast
March 1955	Varnay, Thebom,	
	Svanholm, Hines	
	Metropolitan Opera	
	Orchestra & Chorus	
	Kempe	

TRADITIONAL AND FOLKSONGS

An der Weser

Berlin	Berlin SO	45: Electrola 7EG 8092
June 1954	Schüchter	LP: Electrola VP 8070/SMVP 8070
		LP: EMI 1C 137 769 1901
		CD: EMI CDM 763 6742

Ich schiess' den Hirsch im wilden Forst

Berlin	Berlin SO	45: Electrola 7EG 8092
June 1954	Schüchter	LP: Electrola VP 8070/SMVP 8070
		LP: EMI 1C 137 769 1901

MÜNCHNER OPERNFESTSPIELE

München, Sonntag, 11. August 1957

URAUFFÜHRUNG

Die Harmonie der Welt

Oper in fünf Aufzügen

Text und Musik von PAUL HINDEMITH

Musikalische Leitung: Der Komponist   Bühnenbild: Helmut Jürgens

Inszenierung: Rudolf Hartmann

Kaiser Rudolf II. — Sol	Kieth Engen
Kaiser Ferdinand II.	Karl Hoppe
Johannes Kepler, kaiserlicher Mathematiker — Erde	Josef Metternich
Wallenstein, Feldherr — Jupiter	Richard Holm
Ulrich Grüsser, Keplers Gehilfe; später Soldat — Mars	Kurt Wehofschitz
Daniel Hitzler, Pfarrer in Linz — Ein Regensburger Pfarrer — Merkur	Josef Knapp
Tansur — Saturn	Marcel Cordes
Baron Starhemberg	Max Proebstl
Christoph, Keplers Bruder	Franz Klarwein
Susanna, später Keplers Frau — Venus	Liselotte Fölser
Katharina, Keplers Mutter — Luna	Hertha Töpper
Die kleine Susanna, Keplers Töchterchen aus erster Ehe	Luise Camer
Vogt	Albrecht Peter
Anwalt	Rudolf Wünzer
	Karl Ostertag
Drei Mörder	Rudolf Wünzer
	Adolf Kell

Volk, Soldaten, Sternbilder

Die Handlung spielt zwischen 1608 und 1630

Hermann Uhde
1914-1965

Discography compiled by John Hunt

LUDWIG VAN BEETHOVEN (1770-1827)

Fidelio

New York February 1960	Role of Pizarro Nilsson, Hurley, Vickers, Anthony, Czerwenka, Tozzi Metropolitan Opera Orchestra & Chorus Böhm	LP: Melodram MEL 045 Excerpt LP: Melodram MEL 094

ALBAN BERG (1885-1935)

Wozzeck

New York March 1959	Role of Wozzeck Steber, Roggero, Baum, Anthony, Dönch, Franke Metropolitan Opera Orchestra & Chorus Böhm Sung in English	Unpublished Met broadcast Excerpt LP: Melodram MEL 094

GEORGES BIZET (1838-1875)

Carmen, excerpt (Votre toast)

Stuttgart November 1952	Württembergisches Staatsorchester and Chorus Leitner Sung in German	45: DG NL 32 077

156   Uhde

BORIS BLACHER (1903-1975)

Romeo und Julia

Salzburg August 1950	<u>Role of Capulet</u> Güden, Wagner, Holm, Witt, Böhme Vienna Opera Chorus VPO Krips	Unpublished radio broadcast

BENJAMIN BRITTEN (1913-1976)

The Rape of Lucretia

Salzburg August 1950	<u>Role of Tarquinius</u> Kupper, Güden, Höngen, Patzak, Böhme, Poell VPO Krips	Unpublished radio broadcast

EUGEN D'ALBERT (1864-1932)

Tiefland, excerpt (Hüll' in die Mantille)

Munich June 1953	Munich PO Bavarian Radio Chorus Rother	LP: DG LPE 17 002

CHARLES GOUNOD (1818-1893)

Messe solennelle de Sainte Cécile

Prague June 1965	Seefried, Stolze Czech PO and Chorus Markevitch	LP: DG SLPEM 139 111 LP: Supraphon 50736 CD: DG 427 4092

GEORGE FRIDERIC HANDEL (1685-1759)

Giulio Cesare, excerpt (Dall' ondo periglio/Aure, deh, per pietà!)

Bremen 1937	Bremen RO Eckner <u>Sung in German</u>	LP: Melodram MEL 094
Stuttgart November 1952	Württembergisches Staatsorchester Leitner	45: DG EPL 30 084
Stuttgart November 1952	Württembergisches Staatsorchester Leitner <u>Sung in German</u>	LP: DG LPEM 19 043

WOLFGANG AMADEUS MOZART (1756-1791)

Die Zauberflöte

Salzburg July 1949	<u>Role of 2nd Armed Man</u> Seefried, Lipp, Oravez, W.Ludwig, Schmitt-Walter, Greindl, Schöffler Vienna Opera Chorus VPO Furtwängler	LP: Ed Smith EJS 572 LP: Discocorp IGI 337 LP: Nippon Columbia OZ 7572-7574 LP: Cetra (Japan) GT 7093-7094 CD: Arlecchino ARL 78-80 CD: Music and Arts CD 882
Salzburg August 1950	Seefried, Lipp, Heuser, Dermota, Kunz, Greindl, Schöffler Vienna Opera Chorus VPO Furtwängler	Unpublished radio broadcast <u>Recording survives incomplete</u>

CARL ORFF (1895-1982)

Antigonae

Salzburg August 1949	<u>Role of Kreon</u> Zadek, R.Fischer, Ilosvay, Krebs, Fehenberger, Haefliger, Kusche, Greindl Vienna Opera Chorus VPO Fricsay	CD: Stradivarius STR 10060 <u>World premiere performance</u>
Munich January 1951	Goltz, Schech, Barth, Kuen, Ostertag, Haefliger, Kusche, Böhme Bavarian State Orchestra & Chorus Solti	CD: Orfeo C407 952I <u>Excerpt</u> LP: Melodram MEL 094

Antigonae, scenes 4 and 5

Vienna 1955	Goltz, Rössel-Majdan, Greindl Vienna Opera Chorus VSO Hollreiser	LP: Philips ABL 3316/A01240L

FRANZ SCHUBERT (1797-1828)

Mass in A flat D678

Munich 1965	Stader, Höffgen, Haefliger Regensburger Domchor Bavarian RO Ratzinger	LP: DG SLPEM 139 108

Lieder: Das Rosenband; Geheimnis; Der Jüngling an der Quelle

Bremen 1949	Gehl, piano	LP: Melodram MEL 094

RICHARD STRAUSS (1864-1949)

Die ägyptische Helena

Munich August 1956	Role of Altair Rysanek, Kupper, Aldenhoff, Holm Bavarian State Orchestra & Chorus Keilberth	LP: Ed Smith EJS 268/SP1 LP: Melodram MEL 109 CD: Melodram MEL 27066 CD: Orfeo C423 962I

Arabella

London September 1953	Role of Mandryka Della Casa, Sommerschuh, Fehenberger, Kusche Bavarian State Orchestra & Chorus Kempe	Unpublished radio broadcast Excerpt LP: Melodram MEL 094 Guest performance by Bayerische Staatsoper

Elektra

New York March 1961	Role of Orest Borkh, Rysanek, Madeira, Vinay Metropolitan Opera Orchestra Rosenstock	Unpublished Met broadcast

Elektra, excerpt (Was willst du, fremder Mensch?)

Munich 1955	Goltz Bavarian State Orchestra Böhm	LP: Melodram MEL 094

GIUSEPPE VERDI (1813-1901)

Don Carlo

New York April 1959	<u>Role of Inquisitor</u> Rysanek, Thebom, Gari, Merrill, Hines Metropolitan Opera Orchestra & Chorus Cleva	LP: Melodram MEL 001 <u>Excerpt</u> LP: Melodram MEL 094

Don Carlo, excerpt (Ella giammai m'amò)

Bremen 1937	Bremen RO Eckner <u>Sung in German</u>	LP: Melodram MEL 094

Rigoletto, excerpt (Cortigiani, vil razza dannata!)

Munich June 1953	Munich PO Rother	45: DG EPL 30 084 LP: DG LPE 17 011
Munich June 1953	Munich PO Rother <u>Sung in German</u>	45: DG NL 32 077

Rigoletto, excerpt (Tutte le feste)

Munich June 1953	Streich Munich PO Leitner	LP: DG LPE 17 011
Munich June 1953	Streich Munich PO Leitner <u>Sung in German</u>	LP: DG LPEM 19 043

<u>Rita Streich discography (Teachers and pupils) incorrectly stated that these versions of the Rigoletto duet were recorded in Berlin in October 1953</u>

Caricature of Hermann Uhde from the book
Im Konzertsaal karikiert (Langen-Müller 1959

München, Sonntag, 9. Januar 1955

4. Sonntag-Platzmiete und freier Verkauf

Don Giovanni

Oper in zwei Aufzügen (10 Bildern) von WOLFGANG AMADEUS MOZART

Musikalische Leitung: Robert Heger Regie: Heinz Arnold

Bühnenbild: Helmut Jürgens

Don Giovanni, ein leichtfertiger Edelmann . . . . Hermann Uhde
Donna Anna, Don Ottavios Verlobte . . . . Annelies Kupper
Don Ottavio, ein junger Edelmann . . . . Richard Holm
Der Komtur, Donna Annas Vater . . . . Ferdinand Frantz
Donna Elvira, Dame aus Burgos, von Don
   Giovanni verlassen . . . . Elisabeth Lindermeier
Leporello, Don Giovannis Diener . . . . Gustav Neidlinger a. G.
Masetto, ein junger Bauer . . . . Albrecht Peter
Zerlina, Masettos Braut . . . . Rosl Schwaiger

Bauernburschen und Mädchen, Diener und Musikanten

Die Handlung spielt in Spanien

Einstudierung der Tänze im 5. Bild: Lula v. Sachnovsky
(Solist: Will Spindler)

164 Uhde

RICHARD WAGNER (1813-1883)

Der fliegende Holländer

Bayreuth July 1955	<u>Role of Holländer</u> Varnay, Schärtel, Windgassen, Traxel, Weber Bayreuth Festival Orchestra & Chorus Keilberth	LP: Decca LXT 5150-5152/ECS 665-667/D97 D3 CD: Voce della luna VL 20122 <u>Excerpts</u> LP: Telefunken BLK 16513
Bayreuth July 1955	Varnay, Schärtel, Lustig, Traxel, Weber Bayreuth Festival Orchestra & Chorus Knappertsbusch	LP: Discocorp IGI 319 LP: Cetra LO 51 LP: Melodram MEL 550 CD: Music and Arts CD 319 CD: Hunt CDLSMH 34021 <u>Excerpt</u> LP: Melodram MEL 094

Götterdämmerung

Bayreuth August 1951	<u>Role of Gunther</u> Varnay, Mödl, Schwarzkopf, Höngen, Aldenhoff, Weber, Pflanzl Bayreuth Festival Orchestra & Chorus Knappertsbusch	Decca unpublished
Bayreuth August 1951	Varnay, Mödl, Schwarzkopf, Siewert, Aldenhoff, Weber, Pflanzl Bayreuth Festival Orchestra & Chorus Karajan	Columbia unpublished
Bayreuth August 1952	Varnay, Mödl, Siewert, Lorenz, Greindl, Neidlinger Bayreuth Festival Orchestra & Chorus Keilberth	LP: Melodram MEL 529 CD: Paragon PCD 84025-84028 CD: Arlecchino ARL 55-58
Bayreuth August 1953	Varnay, Malaniuk, Hinsch-Gröndahl, Windgassen, Greindl, Neidlinger Bayreuth Festival Orchestra & Chorus Krauss	LP: Foyer FO 1011 CD: Foyer 4CF 2010/15CF 2011 CD: Rodolphe RPC 32503-32509 CD: Gala GL 999.791/GL 100.159
Bayreuth August 1953	Mödl, Malaniuk, Hinsch-Gröndahl, Windgassen, Greindl, Neidlinger Bayreuth Festival Orchestra & Chorus Keilberth	LP: Allegro-Elite 3138-3142 LP: Melodram MEL 539
Bayreuth August 1955	Varnay, Ilosvay, Brouwenstijn, Windgassen, Greindl, Neidlinger Bayreuth Festival Orchestra & Chorus Keilberth	Decca unpublished

Götterdämmerung/concluded

Munich September 1955	Nilsson, Rysanek, Malaniuk, Aldenhoff, Frick Bavarian State Orchestra & Chorus Knappertsbusch	LP: Melodram MEL 425 CD: Orfeo C356 944L
Bayreuth August 1956	Varnay, Madeira, Brouwenstijn, Windgassen, Greindl, Neidlinger Bayreuth Festival Orchestra & Chorus Knapperstbusch	LP: Melodram MEL 569 CD: Seven Seas (Japan) KICC 2274-2288 CD: Melodram GDM 1001
New York March 1957	Harshaw, Schech, Madeira, Windgassen, Böhme, Davidson Metropolitan Opera Orchestra & Chorus Stiedry	Unpublished Met broadcast Excerpt LP: Melodram MEL 094
Bayreuth August 1957	Varnay, Grümmer, Ilosvay, Windgassen, Greindl, Neidlinger Bayreuth Festival Orchestra & Chorus Knappertsbusch	LP: Estro armonico EA 034 LP: Discocorp IGI 292 LP: Cetra LO 61/DOC 50 LP: Melodram MEL 579 CD: Music and Arts CD 256 CD: Laudis LCD 44013/154 020
London October 1957	Nilsson, Ilosvay, Lindermeier, Svanholm, Frick, Kraus Covent Garden Orchestra & Chorus Kempe	Unpublished radio broadcast

Lohengrin

Bayreuth August 1953	Role of Telramund Steber, Varnay, Windgassen, Greindl, Braun Bayreuth Festival Orchestra & Chorus Keilberth	LP: Decca LXT 2880-2884/D12 D5 CD: Teldec 4509 936742
Bayreuth August 1954	Nilsson, Varnay, Windgassen, Adam, Fischer-Dieskau Bayreuth Festival Orchestra & Chorus Jochum	LP: Cetra LO 77 LP: Melodram MEL 541 CD: Laudis LCD 44015 CD: Melodram MEL 36104 Excerpts LP: Gioielli della lirica GML 20 CD: Memories HR 4275-4276
New York December 1955	Steber, Harshaw, Sullivan, Budney, Edelmann Metropolitan Opera Orchestra & Chorus Stiedry	Unpublished Met broadcast

BAYREUTHER FESTSPIELE · DIENSTAG, 16. AUGUST 1955 · PARSIFAL
EIN BÜHNENWEIHFESTSPIEL VON RICHARD WAGNER

AMFORTAS	DIETRICH FISCHER-DIESKAU
TITUREL	HERMANN UHDE
GURNEMANZ	LUDWIG WEBER
PARSIFAL	RAMON VINAY
KLINGSOR	GUSTAV NEIDLINGER
KUNDRY	MARTHA MÖDL
1. GRALSRITTER	JOSEF TRAXEL
2. GRALSRITTER	ALFONS HERWIG
1. KNAPPE	PAULA LENCHNER
2. KNAPPE	ELISABETH SCHÄRTEL
3. KNAPPE	GERHARD STOLZE
4. KNAPPE	ALFRED PFEIFLE
1. BLUME I. GRUPPE	ILSE HOLLWEG
2. BLUME I. GRUPPE	FRIEDL PÖLTINGER
3. BLUME I. GRUPPE	PAULA LENCHNER
1. BLUME II. GRUPPE	DOROTHEA SIEBERT
2. BLUME II. GRUPPE	JUTTA VULPIUS
3. BLUME II. GRUPPE	ELISABETH SCHÄRTEL
DIRIGENT	HANS KNAPPERTSBUSCH
REGIE UND INSZENIERUNG	WIELAND WAGNER
CHÖRE	WILHELM PITZ
CHOREOGRAPHIE UND REGIEASSISTENZ	GERTRUD WAGNER
KOSTÜME	KURT PALM
BELEUCHTUNG UND TECHN. BERATUNG	PAUL EBERHARDT
MASKENBILDNER	WILLI KLOSE
MUSIKALISCHE EINSTUDIERUNG	WALTER BORN
BELEUCHTUNGSANSAGE	RUDOLF JOHN
AUSSTATTUNGSLEITUNG	OTTO WISSNER
TECHNISCHE BÜHNENLEITUNG	ARTUR EISENSCHMIDT

DER BEGINN JEDES AKTES WIRD 15 MINUTEN VORHER MIT EINER FANFARE, 10 MINUTEN VORHER MIT ZWEI UND 5 MINUTEN VORHER MIT DREI FANFAREN ANGEKÜNDIGT
1. AUFZUG 16 UHR · 2. AUFZUG 18.50 UHR · 3. AUFZUG 21.00 UHR · ENDE GEGEN 22.20 UHR · NACH BEGINN DER AUFZÜGE KEIN EINLASS

BAYREUTHER FESTSPIELE

FREITAG, 22. JULI 1955

RICHARD WAGNER
DER FLIEGENDE HOLLÄNDER
ROMANTISCHE OPER IN DREI AKTEN

DALAND, EIN NORWEGISCHER SEEFAHRER	LUDWIG WEBER
SENTA, SEINE TOCHTER	ASTRID VARNAY
ERIK, EIN JÄGER	WOLFGANG WINDGASSEN
MARY, SENTAS AMME	ELISABETH SCHÄRTEL
DER STEUERMANN DALANDS	JOSEF TRAXEL
DER HOLLÄNDER	HERMANN UHDE
MATROSEN DES NORWEGERS	DIE MANNSCHAFT
DES FLIEGENDEN HOLLÄNDERS	MÄDCHEN
SZENE:	DIE NORWEGISCHE KÜSTE

DIRIGENT	HANS KNAPPERTSBUSCH
REGIE UND INSZENIERUNG	WOLFGANG WAGNER
CHÖRE	WILHELM PITZ
MUSIKALISCHE EINSTUDIERUNG	PAUL ZELTER
KOSTÜME	KURT PALM
AUSSTATTUNGSLEITUNG	OTTO WISSNER
MASKEN	WILLI KLOSE
BELEUCHTUNG	PAUL EBERHARDT
TECHN. BÜHNENLEITUNG	ARTUR EISENSCHMIDT

DER BEGINN DER AUFFÜHRUNG WIRD 15 MINUTEN VORHER MIT EINER FANFARE, 10 MINUTEN VORHER MIT ZWEI UND 5 MINUTEN VORHER MIT DREI FANFAREN ANGEKÜNDIGT · BEGINN 19 UHR · ENDE GEGEN 21.25 UHR · NACH BEGINN DER AUFFÜHRUNG KEIN EINLASS

Parsifal

Bayreuth August 1951	Role of Klingsor Mödl, Windgassen, London, Weber, Van Mill Bayreuth Festival Orchestra & Chorus Knappertsbusch	LP: Decca LXT 2651-2656/GOM 504-508/ 411 7861 LP: London LLPA 10/RS 65001 CD: Decca 425 9762 CD: Teldec 9031 760472 Excerpts 78: Decca (Germany) SX 63018-63030 LP: Telefunken ND 523 425 9762 was not actually published
Bayreuth August 1953	Mödl, Vinay, London, Weber, Greindl Bayreuth Festival Orchestra & Chorus Krauss	LP: Documents OR 305 LP: Melodram MEL 533 LP: Rodolphe RP 12378-12381 CD: Rodolphe RPC 32516-32517 CD: Laudis LCD 44006 CD: Arlecchino ARLA 18-21 Excerpts LP: Melodram MEL 650
New York March 1956	Role of Amfortas Harshaw, Sullivan, Edelmann, Pechner, Moscona Metropolitan Opera Orchestra & Chorus Stiedry	Unpublished Met broadcast Excerpt LP: Melodram MEL 094 Uhde's voice is clearly heard in this excerpt (Wehvolles Erbe!), although Metropolitan Opera Annals state that role of Amfortas was sung in 1956 performances by Paul Schöffler

Das Rheingold

Bayreuth July 1952	Role of Wotan Borkh, Malaniuk, Windgassen, Witte, Kuen, Weber, Greindl, Neidlinger Bayreuth Festival Orchestra Keilberth	LP: Melodram MEL 526 CD: Paragon PCD 84015-84016 CD: Arlecchino ARL 29-30
New York January 1957	Moll, Madeira, Vinay, McCracken, Budney, Pechner, Böhme, Ernster Metropolitan Opera Orchestra Stiedry	Unpublished Met broadcast Excerpt LP: Melodram MEL 094
Bayreuth August 1960	Bjoner, Töpper, Paskuda, Stolze, H.Kraus, O.Kraus, Stewart, Van Mill, Roth-Ehrang Bayreuth Festival Orchestra Kempe	LP: Melodram MEL 606
Bayreuth July 1953	Role of Donner Falcon, Malaniuk, Stolze, Witte, Neidlinger, Weber, Greindl Bayreuth Festival Orchestra Krauss	LP: Foyer FO 1008 CD: Foyer 3CF 2007/15CF 2011 CD: Rodolphe RPC 32503-32509 CD: Gala GL 999.791/GL 100.159
Bayreuth August 1953	Falcon, Malaniuk, Witte, Stolze, Neidlinger, Weber, Greindl Bayreuth Festival Orchestra Keilberth	LP: Allegro-Elite 3125-3127 LP: Melodram MEL 536

172 Uhde

Siegfried

Bayreuth July 1960	Role of Wanderer Nilsson, Siebert, Höffgen, Hopf, H.Kraus, O.Kraus, Roth-Ehrang Bayreuth Festival Orchestra Kempe	LP: Melodram MEL 608 Excerpt LP: Melodram MEL 094

Tristan und Isolde

	Role of Melot Mödl, Malaniuk, Vinay, Hotter, Weber Bayreuth Festival Orchestra & Chorus Karajan	LP: Discocorp IGI 291 LP: Cetra LO 47 LP: Foyer FO 1038 LP: Melodram MEL 525 CD: Hunt CD 528 CD: Myto MCD 962.149

Die Walküre, extracts (Nun zäume dein Ross!; Der alte Sturm, die alte Müh'!; Nimm' den Eid!; Zurück von dem Speer!...to end of Act 2; Wo ist Brünnhild', wo die Verbrecherin?...to end of opera)

New York February 1957	Role of Wotan Schech, Harshaw, Thebom, Vinay, Scott Metropolitan Opera Orchestra & Chorus Mitropoulos	LP: Metropolitan Opera Record Club MO 728 Wotan's Farewell LP: Melodram MEL 094 These extracts were not from a Met broadcast but were made under studio conditions

RUDOLF WAGNER-REGENY (1903-1969)

Das Bergwerk zu Falun

Salzburg August 1961	Role of Fröbom Schwarzenberg, R.Fischer, Lorenz, Welter Vienna Opera Chorus VPO Wallberg	Unpublished radio broadcast World premiere performance

CARL MARIA VON WEBER (1786-1826)

Der Freischütz, excerpt (Hier im ird'schen Jammertal)

Bremen 1937	Bremen RO Eckner	LP: Melodram MEL 094
Munich January 1954	Bamberg SO Leitner	LP: DG LPEM 19 013/89 537

Der Freischütz, excerpt (Schweig', damit dich niemand warnt!)

Munich January 1954	Bamberg SO Leitner	LP: DG LPEM 19 013/89 537

Eberhard Wächter
1929-1992

Discography compiled by John Hunt

LUDWIG VAN BEETHOVEN (1770-1827)

Fidelio

Vienna May 1962	Role of Fernando C.Ludwig, Janowitz, Vickers, Kmennt, Kreppel, Berry Vienna Opera Chorus VPO Karajan	LP: Movimento musica 03.014

An die ferne Geliebte, song cycle

Vienna 1957	H.Schmidt	LP: DG LPE 17 112

Gellert-Lieder

Vienna 1957	H.Schmidt	LP: DG LPE 17 112

ALBAN BERG (1885-1935)

Wozzeck

Vienna October- November 1980	Role of Wozzeck Silja, Winkler, Zednik, Malta, Laubenthal Vienna Opera Chorus VPO Dohnanyi	LP: Decca D321 D2 CD: Decca 417 3482

178 Wächter

IRVING BERLIN (1888-1989)

Annie Get Your Gun, excerpt (There's no business like show business!)

Vienna 1957	Lewis, Lorenz, Zimmer Austrian RO Paulik	CD: Myto MCD 93488

GEORGES BIZET (1838-1875)

Carmen, Querschnitt

Cologne 1961	<u>Role of Escamillo</u> Malaniuk, Fahberg, Konya WDR Orchestra and Chorus Marszalek <u>Sung in German</u>	45: Polydor EPH 21402/SEPH 224402 LP: Polydor LPHM 46541/SLPHM 237 041

JOHANNES BRAHMS (1833-1897)

Ein deutsches Requiem

Vienna May 1964	Janowitz Wiener Singverein BPO Karajan	LP: DG KL 33-39/SKL 133-139/2707 018/ 2726 078/2726 505 CD: DG 427 2522
Vienna June 1968	Lipp Wiener Singverein VPO Klemperer	CD: Refrain DR 920034

Liebeslieder-Walzer

Vienna February 1962	Seefried, Kostia, Kmennt Werba, Weissenborn	LP: DG LPM 18 792/SPLM 138 792

Neue Liebeslieder-Walzer

Vienna February 1962	Seefried, Kostia, Kmennt Werba, Weissenborn	LP: DG LPM 18 792/SLPM 138 792

PETER CORNELIUS (1824-1874)

Der Barbier von Bagdad

London May 1956	Role of 1st Muezzin Schwarzkopf, Hoffman, Gedda, Unger, Prey Chorus Philharmonia Leinsdorf	LP: Columbia 33CX 1400-1401 LP: Columbia (Germany) C 90885-90886 LP: Angel 3553 LP: Regal REG 2047-2048 LP: EMI 1C 147 01448-01449M CD: EMI CMS 565 2842

EUGEN D'ALBERT (1864-1932)

Tiefland

Vienna January 1957	Role of Moruccio Brouwenstijn, Hopf, Kmennt, Schöffler, Czerwenka Vienna Opera Chorus VSO Moralt	LP: Philips A00413-00414L/6768 026 LP: Epic 4SC 6025 CD: Philips 434 7812 Excerpts LP: Philips GL 5672/G03100L

LUIGI DALLOPICCOLA (1904-1975)

Il prigionero

Berlin September 1955	Role of Prisoner Werth, Krebs, Ohlshauser St Hedwig's Choir BPO Rosbaud Sung in German	CD: Hunt CDGI 770
Munich March 1956	Pilarczyk, Krebs, Kreppel Bavarian Radio Orchestra & Chorus Scherchen Sung in German	CD: Stradivarius STR 10034
Vienna June 1971	Poli, English, Bösch Austrian Radio Orchestra & Chorus Melles	LP: CBS 61344

Job

Cologne April 1955	Steingruber, C.Ludwig, Wilhelm, Fiedler WDR Orchestra and Chorus Sanzogno	Unpublished radio broadcast

5 canti sacri

Cologne November 1957	WDR Chorus Prausnitz	Unpublished radio broadcast

CLAUDE DEBUSSY (1862-1918)

Pelléas et Mélisande

Vienna January 1962	Role of Golaud Güden, Höngen, H.Gui, Zaccaria, Poell Vienna Opera Chorus VPO Karajan	Unpublished radio broadcast

GAETONO DONIZETTI (1797-1848)

L'elisir d'amore

Vienna May 1973	<u>Role of Dulcamara</u> Grist, Gedda, Kerns Vienna Opera Chorus VPO Varviso	LP: Melodiya M10 47035 004

La favorita, excerpt (Vien, Leonora, a piedi tuoi!)

Berlin November 1957	Berlin RO König <u>Sung in German</u>	45: DG EPL 30 328 LP: Preiser PR 135 015

GOTTFRIED VON EINEM (1918-1996)

Der Besuch der alten Dame

Vienna May 1971	<u>Role of Ill</u> C.Ludwig, Loose, Beirer, Hotter Vienna Opera Chorus VPO Stein	LP: Amadeo 419 5521 CD: Amadeo 419 5522

CHRISTOPH WILLIBALD GLUCK (1714-1787)

Iphigénie en Tauride, excerpt (La malheur en tous lieux suit mes pas/De noirs pressentiments)

Berlin November 1957	Berlin RO König Sung in German	LP: Preiser PR 135 015

Iphigénie en Tauride, excerpt (De tes forfaits la trame est découverte!)

Berlin November 1957	Berlin RO König Sung in German	LP: Preiser PR 135 015

CHARLES GOUNOD (1818-1893)

Faust, excerpt (Avant de quitter ces lieux)

Munich February 1957	Munich PO Leitner	45: DG EPL 30 339 LP: Preiser PR 135 015
Munich February 1957	Munich PO Leitner Sung in German	45: DG EPL 30 338 LP: DG LPEM 19 095/89 651

Faust, excerpt (Par ici, par ici, mes amis!)

Munich February 1957	Stader, Naaf Bavarian Radio Chorus Munich PO Leitner	LP: Preiser PR 135 015
Munich February 1957	Stader, Naaf Bavarian Radio Chorus Munich PO Leitner Sung in German	45: DG EPL 30 328 LP: DG LPEM 19 095/89 651

ENGELBERT HUMPERDINCK (1854-1921)

Königskinder, excerpt (Verdorben! Gestorben!)

Berlin November 1957	Berlin RO König	45: DG EPL 30 309 LP: Preiser PR 135 015

CONRADIN KREUTZER (1780-1849)

Das Nachtlager in Granada, excerpt (Ein Schütz' bin ich in des Regenten Sold)

Berlin November 1957	Berlin RO König	45: DG EPL 30 309 LP: Preiser PR 135 015

FRANZ LEHAR (1870-1948)

Die lustige Witwe

London July 1962	Role of Danilo Schwarzkopf, Steffek, Gedda Philharmonia Orchestra & Chorus Matacic	LP: EMI AN 101-102/SAN 101-102/SLS 823/ 1C153 00001-00002/2C153 00001-00002 LP: Angel 3630 CD: EMI CDS 747 1788 Excerpts LP: EMI ALP 2252/ASD 2252/SHZE 181 LP: Angel 36340

Der Graf von Luxemburg

Munich 1974	Sukis, Kunz Graunke Orchestra Goldschmidt	VHS Video: Taurus 886 Excerpts LP: Philips 6449 084/6623 118 CD: Philips 420 6632

RUGGIERO LEONCAVALLO (1858-1919)

I pagliacci, Querschnitt

Cologne 1961	Role of Tonio Hollweg, Konya WDR Orchestra Marszalek Sung in German	LP: Polydor LPHM 46650/SLPHM 237 150

I pagliacci, excerpt (Nedda! Silvio! A quest' ora che imprudenza)

Berlin November 1957	Schlemm Berlin RO König Sung in German	LP: DG LPEM 19 199 LP: Preiser PR 135 015

FRANZ LISZT (1811-1886)

Die heilige Elisabeth, excerpt (Aus dem Nebel der Täler erschalle hervor!)

Berlin November 1957	Berlin RO König	45: DG EPL 30 303

Die 3 Zigeuner

Berlin November 1957	Berlin RO König	45: DG EPL 30 303

Es muss ein Wunderbares sein

Berlin November 1957	Berlin RO König	45: DG EPL 30 303

CARL LOEWE (1796-1869)

Der Edelfalk

Vienna	Dokoupil	LP: Preiser SPR 3211
1969		CD: Preiser 93211

Erlkönig

Vienna	H.Schmidt	LP: Amadeo AVRS 6257
1957		CD: Sony (Austria) 471 9112

Der gefangene Admiral

Vienna	Dokoupil	LP: Preiser SPR 3211
1969		CD: Preiser 93211

Die Glocken zu Speyer

Vienna	Dokoupil	LP: Preiser SPR 3211
1969		CD: Preiser 93211

Graf Eberhards Weissdorn

Vienna	Dokoupil	LP: Preiser SPR 3211
1969		CD: Preiser 93211

Gregor auf dem Stein

Vienna	Dokoupil	LP: Preiser SPR 3211
1969		CD: Preiser 93211

Loewe Ballads/concluded

Harald

Vienna 1969	Dokoupil	CD: Preiser 93211

Die Kaiserjagd im Wienerwald

Vienna 1969	Dokoupil	CD: Preiser 93211

Landgraf Ludwig

Vienna 1969	Dokoupil	CD: Preiser 93211

Der Mönch zu Pisa

Vienna 1969	Dokoupil	LP: Preiser SPR 3211 CD: Preiser 93211

Die nächtliche Heerschau

Vienna 1969	Dokoupil	CD: Preiser 89230

Odins Meeresritt

Vienna 1957	H.Schmidt	LP: Amadeo AVRS 6257 CD: Sony (Austria) 471 9112

Der Schatzgräber

Vienna 1969	Dokoupil	CD: Preiser 93211

ALBERT LORTZING (1801-1851)

Zar und Zimmermann, Querschnitt

Vienna 1961	Role of Zar Peter Holm, Kmennt, Welter Vienna Volksoper Orchestra & Chorus Bauer-Theussl	LP: Eurodisc 201 587.250/200 417.241/ 300 645.370/KR 72614/KR 72615
Vienna 1963	Güden, Kmennt, Vienna Opera Chorus Volksoper Orchestra Ronnefeld	LP: Decca LXT 6039/SXL 6039/SXL 20532B

PIETRO MASCAGNI (1863-1945)

Cavalleria rusticana

Berlin 1960	Role of Alfio Hillebrecht, Jasper, Schock Deutsche Oper Orchestra & Chorus Hollreiser Sung in German	LP: Eurodisc XDR 27272/XR 72245/ 201 030.250 Excerpts LP: Eurodisc KR 72238/KR 72239/KR 72614/ KR 72615/200 417.241

KARL MILLOECKER (1842-1899)

Der Bettelstudent

Vienna   Role of Janicki   LP: Vanguard PVL 7056-7057
1956   Lipp, Rethy,
            Christ, Preger,
            Dönch
            Vienna Opera Chorus
            VPO
            Paulik

CLAUDIO MONTEVERDI (1567-1643)

L'Orfeo, excerpts

Munich   Role of Orfeo   LP: Gioielli della lirica GML 79
April 1954   Lindermeier,
            L.Fischer, Böhme
            Bavarian Radio
            Orchestra & Chorus
            Jochum

WOLFGANG AMADEUS MOZART (1756-1791)

Don Giovanni

London October 1959	Role of Giovanni Schwarzkopf, Sutherland, Sciutti, Alva, Taddei, Frick, Cappuccilli Philharmonia Orchestra & Chorus Klemperer	Columbia unpublished Recording incomplete
London October 1959	Schwarzkopf, Sutherland, Sciutti, Alva, Taddei, Frick, Cappuccilli Philharmonia Orchestra & Chorus C.Davis	Unpublished radio broadcast

London
October-
November
1959
	Schwarzkopf,
	Sutherland,
	Sciutti, Alva,
	Taddei, Frick,
	Cappuccilli
	Philharmonia
	Orchestra & Chorus
	Giulini
		LP: Columbia 33CX 1717-1720/
		    SAX 2369-2372
		LP: Columbia (Germany) C 91059-91062/
		    STC 91059-91062
		LP: Angel 3605
		LP: EMI 1C 181 00504-00507/SLS 5083
		CD: EMI CDS 747 2608
		<u>Excerpts</u>
		LP: Columbia 33CX 1918/SAX 2559
		LP: Angel 36948
		LP: EMI 1C 061 02056/1C 063 00372/
		    SXLP 30300/SHZE 121
		CD: EMI CDM 763 0782/CDCFP 9013

Don Giovanni/concluded

Lisbon January 1960	Caballé, Otto, Stich-Randall, Kmennt, Kunz, Peter, H.Hoffmann San Carlos Orchestra & Chorus Gielen	CD: Legato SRO 813
Salzburg August 1960	Schwarzkopf, L.Price, Sciutti, Valletti, Berry, Panerai, Zaccaria Vienna Opera Chorus VPO Karajan	LP: Historical Recording Enterprises HRE 247 LP: Movimento musica 03.001 CD: Movimento musica 013.6012 CD: Curcio-Hunt OP 6 CD: Hunt CDKAR 225 Excerpts CD: Orfeo C394 201B/C408 955R
Vienna June 1963	Güden, L.Price, Sciutti, Berry, Wunderlich, Panerai, Kreppel Vienna Opera Chorus VPO Karajan	CD: Verona 27065-27067
Buenos Aires September 1963	Lipp, Grümmer, Scovotti, Alva, G.Evans, Catena, Crass Teatro Colon Orchestra & Chorus Schmidt-Isserstedt	CD: Ornamenti FE 116
Vienna May 1955	Role of Masetto Jurinac, Zadek, Sciutti, Simoneau, London, Weber, Ernster Chamber Choir VSO Moralt	LP: Philips ABL 3069-3071/GL 5753-5755/ A00280-00282L/6768 033 CD: Philips 438 6742 Excerpts LP: Philips GO3068L/695 058KL

STAATSOPER

Mittwoch, den 21. Jänner 1959
Im Abonnement XI. Gruppe. Beschränkter Kartenverkauf

Die Zauberflöte

Oper in zwei Akten von E. Schikaneder

Musik von W. A. Mozart

Musikalische Leitung: Berislav Klobučar
Inszenierung: Günther Rennert
Bühnenbilder und Kostüme: Georges Wakhewitsch
Einstudierung der Chöre: Richard Rossmayer

Sarastro	Gottlob Frick
Königin der Nacht	Mimi Coertse
Pamina, ihre Tochter	Irmgard Seefried
Erste ⎫	Judith Hellwig
Zweite ⎬ Dame der Königin	Margareta Sjöstedt
Dritte ⎭	Hilde Rössel-Majdan
Tamino	Waldemar Kmentt
Papageno	Walter Berry
Papagena	Anneliese Rothenberger
Sprecher	Eberhard Wächter
Monostatos	Peter Klein
Erster ⎫ Priester	Erich Majkut
Zweiter ⎭	Hans Schweiger
Zwei geharnischte Männer	László Szemere / Adolf Vogel
Erster ⎫	
Zweiter ⎬ Knabe	Wiener Sängerknaben
Dritter ⎭	

Technische Einrichtung: Hans Felkel
Beleuchtung: Albin Rotter

Pause nach dem ersten Akt

Anfang 19 Uhr   Ende etwa 22 Uhr

STAATSOPER

Dienstag, den 7. Oktober 1958
Im Abonnement IV. Gruppe. Beschränkter Kartenverkauf

Wegen plötzlicher Erkrankung von Herrn Kammersänger Josef Greindl hat sich Herr Kammersänger Ludwig Weber in liebenswürdiger Weise bereit erklärt, die Rolle des „Veit Pogner" zu übernehmen

Die Meistersinger von Nürnberg

Oper in drei Aufzügen von Richard Wagner

Musikalische Leitung: Heinrich Hollreiser
Inszenierung: Herbert Graf
Bühnenbilder und Kostüme: Robert Kautsky
Einstudierung der Chöre: Richard Rossmayer

Hans Sachs, Schuster		Otto Edelmann
Veit Pogner, Goldschmied		Ludwig Weber
Kunz Vogelgesang, Kürschner		Hugo Meyer-Welfing
Konrad Nachtigall, Spengler		Hans Schweiger
Sixtus Beckmesser, Stadtschreiber		Erich Kunz
Fritz Kothner, Bäcker	Meister-	Eberhard Wächter
Balthasar Zorn, Zinngießer	singer	Erich Majkut
Ulrich Eißlinger, Würzkrämer		Fritz Sperlbauer
Augustin Moser, Schneider		Kurt Equiluz
Hermann Ortel, Seifensieder		Harald Pröglhöf
Hans Schwarz, Strumpfwirker		Franz Bierbach
Hans Foltz, Kupferschmied		Ljubo Pantscheff

Walther v. Stolzing, ein junger Ritter aus
   Franken . . . . Wolfgang Windgassen
David, Sachsens Lehrbube . . . . Anton Dermota
Eva, Pogners Tochter . . . . Elisabeth Grümmer
Magdalena, Evas Amme . . . . Hilde Rössel-Majdan
Ein Nachtwächter . . . . Norman Foster

Bürger und Frauen aller Zünfte, Gesellen, Lehrbuben, Mädchen, Volk

Schauplatz der Handlung: Nürnberg. Um die Mitte des 16. Jahrhunderts

Erster Aufzug: Im Innern der Katharinenkirche — Zweiter Aufzug: In den Straßen vor den Häusern Pogners und Sachsens — Dritter Aufzug: a) Sachsens Werkstatt, b) ein freier Wiesenplan an der Pegnitz

Idomeneo

Salzburg July 1956	Role of Arbace Hillebrecht, Goltz, Schock, Kmennt, Böhme Vienna Opera Chorus VPO Böhm	LP: Movimento musica 03.017 CD: Movimento musica 051.044
Salzburg July 1961	Role of High Priest Lorengar, Grümmer, Kmennt, Haefliger, Capecchi Vienna Opera Chorus VPO Fricsay	LP: Melodram MEL 701 CD: DG 447 6622

Le nozze di Figaro

London
September–
November
1959
	Role of Count
	Schwarzkopf,
	Moffo, Cossotto,
	Taddei
	Philharmonia
	Orchestra & Chorus
	Giulini
		LP: Columbia 33CX 1732-1735/
		    SAX 2381-2384
		LP: Columbia (Germany) C 91184-91186/
		    STC 91184-91186
		LP: Angel 3608
		LP: EMI SLS 5152
		Excerpts
		LP: Columbia 33CX 1934/SAX 2573
		LP: EMI 1C 063 00839/SXLP 30303
		CD: EMI CDM 763 4092

Die Zauberflöte

Vienna May 1962	Role of Sprecher Lipp, Hallstein, Sciutti, Gedda, Kunz, Frick Vienna Opera Chorus VPO Karajan	LP: Movimento musica 03.015 CD: Movimento musica 051.028
Vienna 1963	Mechera, Holm, Wilhelm, Crass Wiener Singverein VSO Sawallisch	Unpublished video recording

Die Zauberflöte, excerpt (Wo willst du, kühner Fremdling, hin?)

Vienna 1970	Dermota VPO Krips	CD: Melodram CDM 26522

OTTO NICOLAI (1810-1849)

Die lustigen Weiber von Windsor, excerpt (In einem Waschkorb?)

| Munich April 1955 | Borg Munich PO Leitner | 45: DG EPL 30 277 LP: DG LPEM 19 049/89 648 LP: Preiser PR 135 015 |

JACQUES OFFENBACH (1819-1880)

La vie parisienne

| Berlin February 1968 | Role of Gondremarck Della Casa, Hallstein, Schramm, Schock, Gruber, Unger, Bohme Deutsche Oper Chorus Berlin SO Allers Sung in German | LP: Eurodisc XE 77485/XF 77489 Excerpts LP: Eurodisc IE 89889/301 115.435 CD: RCA/BMG GD 69020 |

GIACOMO PUCCINI (1858-1924)

Tosca, Querschnitt

| Vienna 1961 | Role of Scarpia Scheyrer, Kmennt Volksoper Orchestra Bauer-Theussl Sung in German | LP: Eurodisc KR 70018/KR 70019/KR 72614/ KR 72615/XBR 25965/200 417.241 |

GIOACHINO ROSSINI (1792-1868)

Il barbiere di Siviglia

Vienna April 1966	Role of Figaro Grist,H.Konetzni, Wunderlich, Kunz, Czerwenka Vienna Opera Chorus VPO Böhm Sung in German	LP: Teatro dischi TD 502-503 CD: Myto MCD 91752 Teatro dischi incorrectly dated 1965

Il barbiere di Siviglia, Querschnitt

Munich November 1964	Hallstein, Kmennt, Kusche, Frick Bavarian State Orchestra Löwlein Sung in German	LP: Eurodisc KR 71872/KR 71873/ KR 86802/KR 72614/KR 72615/ 200 417/241/201 586.250/300 645.370/ XC 28020/XF 79915/XF 86835

ROBERT SCHUMANN (1810-1856)

Allnächtlich im Traume/Dichterliebe

Vienna September 1961	Brendel	LP: Decca LXT 5675/SXL 2310 CD: Decca 425 9492

Die alten bösen Lieder/Dichterliebe

Vienna September 1961	Brendel	LP: Decca LXT 5675/SXL 2310 CD: Decca 425 9492

Am leuchtenden Sommermorgen/Dichterliebe

Vienna September 1961	Brendel	LP: Decca LXT 5675/SXL 2310 CD: Decca 425 9492

Aus alten Märchen winkt es/Dichterliebe

Vienna September 1961	Brendel	LP: Decca LXT 5675/SXL 2310 CD: Decca 425 9492

Aus meinen Tränen spriessen/Dichterliebe

Vienna 1957	H.Schmidt	LP: Amadeo AVRS 6257 CD: Sony (Austria) 471 9112
Vienna September 1961	Brendel	LP: Decca LXT 5675/SXL 2310 CD: Decca 425 9492

Das ist ein Flöten und Geigen/Dichterliebe

Vienna September 1961	Brendel	LP: Decca LXT 5675/SXL 2310 CD: Decca 425 9492

Schumann Lieder/continued

Hör' ich das Liedchen klingen/Dichterliebe

Vienna September 1961	Brendel	LP: Decca LXT 5675/SXL 2310 CD: Decca 425 9492

Ich grolle nicht/Dichterliebe

Vienna September 1961	Brendel	LP: Decca LXT 5675/SXL 2310 CD: Decca 425 9492

Ich hab' im Traum geweinet/Dichterliebe

Vienna September 1961	Brendel	LP: Decca LXT 5675/SXL 2310 CD: Decca 425 9492

Ich will meine Seele tauchen/Dichterliebe

Vienna September 1961	Brendel	LP: Decca LXT 5675/SXL 2310 CD: Decca 425 9492

Im Rhein, im heiligen Strome/Dichterliebe

Vienna September 1961	Brendel	LP: Decca LXT 5675/SXL 2310 CD: Decca 425 9492

Im wunderschönen Monat Mai/Dichterliebe

Vienna September 1961	Brendel	LP: Decca LXT 5675/SXL 2310 CD: Decca 425 9492

Schumann Lieder/continued

In der Fremde/Liederkreis op 39 (Aus der Heimat hinter den Blitzen rot)

Vienna 1957	H.Schmidt	LP: Amadeo AVRS 6257 CD: Sony (Austria) 471 9112

Ein Jüngling liebt ein Mädchen/Dichterliebe

Vienna September 1961	Brendel	LP: Decca LXT 5675/SXL 2310 CD: Decca 425 9492

Lehn' deine Wang' an meine Wang'

Vienna 1957	H.Schmidt	LP: Amadeo AVRS 6257 CD: Sony (Austria) 471 9112
Vienna September 1961	Brendel	LP: Decca LXT 5675/SXL 2310 CD: Decca 425 9492

Mein Wagen rollet langsam

Vienna 1957	H.Schmidt	LP: Amadeo AVRS 6257 CD: Sony (Austria) 471 9112
Vienna September 1961	Brendel	LP: Decca LXT 5675/SXL 2310 CD: Decca 425 9492

Mit Myrthen und Rosen/Liederkreis op 24

Vienna 1957	H.Schmidt	LP: Amadeo AVRS 6257 CD: Sony (Austria) 471 9112
Vienna September 1961	Brendel	LP: Decca LXT 5675/SXL 2310 CD: Decca 425 9492

Schumann Lieder/concluded

Die Rose, die Lilie, die Taube, die Sonne/Dichterliebe

Vienna September 1961	Brendel	LP: Decca LXT 5675/SXL 2310 CD: Decca 425 9492

Schöne Wiege meiner Leiden/Liederkreis op 24

Vienna 1957	H.Schmidt	LP: Amadeo AVRS 6257 CD: Sony (Austria) 471 9112
Vienna September 1961	Brendel	LP: Decca LXT 5675/SXL 2310 CD: Decca 425 9492

Und wüssten's die Blumen/Dichterliebe

Vienna September 1961	Brendel	LP: Decca LXT 5675/SXL 2310 CD: Decca 425 9492

Wenn ich in deine Augen seh'/Dichterliebe

Vienna September 1961	Brendel	LP: Decca LXT 5675/SXL 2310 CD: Decca 425 9492

BEDRICH SMETANA (1824-1884)

Dalibor

Vienna October 1969	Role of King Rysanek, Spiess, Dallapozza Vienna Opera Chorus VPO Krips Sung in German	CD: Myto MCD 92465

ROBERT STOLZ (1880-1975)

Die Rosen der Madonna

Vienna 1973	Role of Pater Clemens Janowitz, Kmennt, Pernerstorfer Austrian RO Stolz	LP: BASF BB 20.212610

JOHANN STRAUSS (1825-1899)

Cagliostro in Wien, Querschnitt

Vienna Date not confirmed	Role of Cagliostro Scheyrer, C.Ludwig, Kmennt Vienna Opera Chorus VSO Salmhofer	LP: Philips A02216L

Die Fledermaus

London
June-
July 1959
	Role of Falke
	Lipp, Scheyrer,
	C.Ludwig, Terkal,
	Berry, Kunz
	Philharmonia
	Orchestra & Chorus
	Ackermann
		LP: Columbia 33CX 1688-1689/
		    SAX 2336-2337
		LP: Columbia (Germany) C 80596-80597/
		    STC 80596-80597/SCXW 7606-7607
		LP: EMI 1C 147 01652-01653/CFPD 4702
		CD: EMI CFPCD 4702
		Excerpts
		LP: EMI XLP 20091/SXLP 20091/
		    1C 183 28811-28813

Vienna July 1960	Role of Frank Güden, Köth, Resnik, Kmennt, Zampieri, Berry, Kunz Vienna Opera Chorus VPO Karajan	LP: Decca MET 201-203/SET 201-203/ LXT 6015-6016/SXL 6015-6016/D247 D3 CD: Decca 421 0462 Excerpts LP: Decca LXT 6155/SXL 6155

Die Fledermaus/concluded

Vienna December 1960	Role of Eisenstein Güden, Streich, Stolze, Zampieri, Kunz, Berry Vienna Opera Chorus VPO Karajan	LP: Foyer FO 1031 CD: Foyer 3CF-2021 CD: Hunt CDKAR 215 Excerpts LP: Gioielli della lirica GML 25
Vienna 1964	Rothenberger, Leigh, Stevens, Konya, Kunz, London Vienna Opera Chorus VPO Danon	LP: Victor LM 7029/LSC 7029 LP: RCA SER 5514-5515/26.35058
Vienna February 1971	Janowitz, Holm, Windgassen, Kunz, Kmennt, Holecek Vienna Opera Chorus VPO Böhm	LP: Decca SET 540-541 VHS Video: Victor (Japan) JHC 0118 VHS Video: Taurus 884 Decca omits dialogue
Munich December 1986	Coburn, Perry, Fassbaender, Brendel, Kusche, Hopferwieser Bavarian State Orchestra & Chorus C.Kleiber	VHS Video: DG 072 4003 Laserdisc: DG 072 4001

Der lustige Krieg, Querschnitt

Vienna Date not confirmed	Roles of Groot and Franchetti Siebert, C.Ludwig, Kmennt Vienna Opera Chorus VSO E.Strauss	LP: Philips A02216L

Ritter Pasman

Vienna 1975	Role of Pasman Ghazarian, T.Schmidt, Korn, Hopferwieser Austrian Radio Orchestra & Chorus Wallberg	LP: Ed Smith UORC 333 Ein schlechter Spass LP: Austrian Radio private issue

Der Zigeunerbaron

Vienna 1957	Role of Carnero Loose, Scheyrer, Kmennt, Kunz, Preger Vienna Opera Chorus VSO Paulik	LP: Philips GL 5724-5725/G04200-04201L LP: Vanguard PVL 7033-7034 LP: Amadeo VRS 486-487/AVRS 6054-6055
Berlin May 1964	Role of Homonay Hazy, Schädle, H.Konetzni, Schock, Schmitt-Walter, Kusche Deutsche Oper Orchestra & Chorus Stolz	Unpublished video recording LP: Eurodisc XE 71454/XE 71455 Excerpts LP: Eurodisc IE 71680/IE 71681/IE 89897/ 200.417 241

ROYAL FESTIVAL HALL

GENERAL MANAGER: T. E. BEAN, C.B.E.

PHILHARMONIA CONCERT SOCIETY LTD

ARTISTIC DIRECTOR:
WALTER LEGGE

CONCERT PERFORMANCE

MOZART
DON GIOVANNI

DRAMMA GIOCOSO IN TWO ACTS

Text by
LORENZO DA PONTE

ONE INTERVAL OF TWENTY MINUTES AFTER THE FIRST ACT

Sunday, 18th October 1959, at 7.30 p.m.
Tuesday, 20th October 1959, at 7.30 p.m.

Programme Two Shillings and Sixpence

DON GIOVANNI

Cast in order of appearance

Leporello, *servant to Don Giovanni*	Giuseppe Taddei
Donna Anna, *betrothed to Don Ottavio*	Joan Sutherland
Don Giovanni, *an extremely licentious young nobleman*	Eberhard Waechter
Il Commendatore, *father of Donna Anna*	Gottlob Frick
Don Ottavio	Luigi Alva
Donna Elvira, *a lady of Burgos, deserted by Don Giovanni*	Elisabeth Schwarzkopf
Zerlina, *a peasant girl, betrothed to Masetto*	Graziella Sciutti
Masetto, *a peasant*	Piero Cappuccilli

PHILHARMONIA ORCHESTRA
Leader: Hugh Bean

Conductor
COLIN DAVIS
(*by permission of Sadler's Wells Opera*)

Members of the
PHILHARMONIA CHORUS
Guest Chorus Master: Roberto Benaglio

Harpsichord Prof. Heinrich Schmidt

Musical Assistants
Prof. Heinrich Schmidt
Mo. Antonio Tonini
Harpsichord by Thomas Goff

LE NOZZE DI FIGARO

Cast in order of appearance

Figaro, *Servant to Conte Almaviva*	Giuseppe Taddei
Susanna, *Maid to Contessa Almaviva*	Anna Moffo
Dr Bartolo	Ivo Vinco
Marcellina, *his former housekeeper*	Dora Gatta
Cherubino, *Page to Conte Almaviva*	Fiorenza Cossotto
Il Conte Almaviva	Eberhard Waechter
Don Basilio, *a Music Teacher*	Renato Ercolani
La Contessa Almaviva	Elisabeth Schwarzkopf
Antonio, *gardener to Conte Almaviva*	Piero Cappuccilli
Barbarina, *his daughter*	Elisabetta Fusco
Don Curzio, *a Notary*	Renato Ercolani
Two Girls	Gillian Spencer
	Diana Gillingham

PHILHARMONIA ORCHESTRA
Leader: Hugh Bean

Conductor
CARLO MARIA GIULINI

Members of the
PHILHARMONIA CHORUS
Guest Chorus Master: Roberto Benaglio

Harpsichord Prof. Heinrich Schmidt

Musical Assistants
Prof. Heinrich Schmidt
Mo. Antonio Tonini

Harpsichord by Thomas Goff

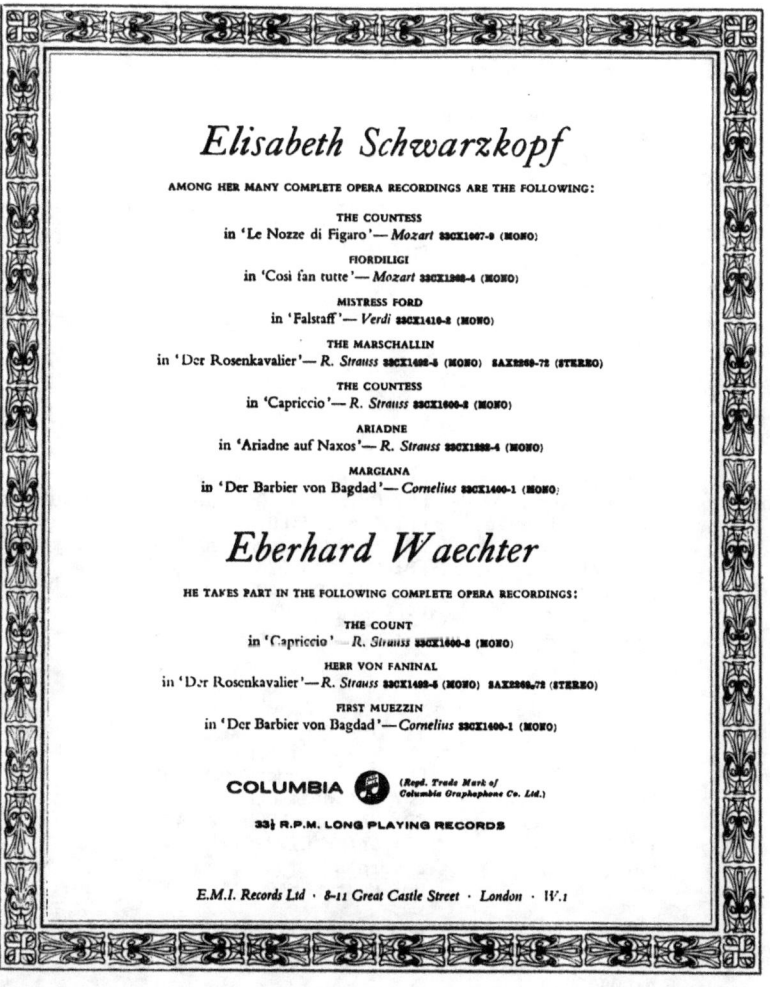

Elisabeth Schwarzkopf

AMONG HER MANY COMPLETE OPERA RECORDINGS ARE THE FOLLOWING:

THE COUNTESS
in 'Le Nozze di Figaro'—*Mozart* 33CX1007-9 (MONO)

FIORDILIGI
in 'Cosi fan tutte'—*Mozart* 33CX1262-4 (MONO)

MISTRESS FORD
in 'Falstaff'—*Verdi* 33CX1410-2 (MONO)

THE MARSCHALLIN
in 'Der Rosenkavalier'—*R. Strauss* 33CX1492-5 (MONO) SAX2269-72 (STEREO)

THE COUNTESS
in 'Capriccio'—*R. Strauss* 33CX1600-2 (MONO)

ARIADNE
in 'Ariadne auf Naxos'—*R. Strauss* 33CX1292-4 (MONO)

MARGIANA
in 'Der Barbier von Bagdad'—*Cornelius* 33CX1400-1 (MONO)

Eberhard Waechter

HE TAKES PART IN THE FOLLOWING COMPLETE OPERA RECORDINGS:

THE COUNT
in 'Capriccio'—*R. Strauss* 33CX1600-2 (MONO)

HERR VON FANINAL
in 'Der Rosenkavalier'—*R. Strauss* 33CX1492-5 (MONO) SAX2269-72 (STEREO)

FIRST MUEZZIN
in 'Der Barbier von Bagdad'—*Cornelius* 33CX1400-1 (MONO)

COLUMBIA (Regd. Trade Mark of Columbia Graphophone Co. Ltd.)

33⅓ R.P.M. LONG PLAYING RECORDS

E.M.I. Records Ltd · 8-11 Great Castle Street · London · W.1

RICHARD STRAUSS (1864-1949)

Arabella

Vienna September 1976	Role of Mandryka Janowitz, Popp, Bence, Dallapozza, Czerwenka Vienna Opera Chorus VPO Hollreiser	VHS Video: Lyric (USA) 8636
Vienna May-June 1957	Role of Dominik Della Casa, Güden, Malaniuk, Dermota, London, Edelmann Vienna Opera Chorus VPO Solti	LP: Decca LXT 5403-5406/SXL 2050-2053/ GOS 571-573 CD: Decca 430 3872

Capriccio

London September 1957	Role of Count Schwarzkopf, Moffo, C.Ludwig, Gedda, Hotter, Fischer-Dieskau, Schmitt-Walter Philharmonia Sawallisch	LP: Columbia 33CX 1600-1602 LP: Columbia (Germany) C 90997-90999 LP: Angel 3580 LP: World Records OC 230-232 LP: EMI 143 5243 CD: EMI CDS 749 0148 Excerpts LP: World Records OH 233

Elektra

Salzburg August 1964	Role of Orest Varnay, Mödl, Hillebrecht, King VPO Karajan	LP: Estro armonico EA 044 LP: Melodram MEL 718 CD: Melodram CDM 27044 CD: Orfeo C298 922I Excerpts CD: Hunt CDKAR 213
Vienna December 1965	Nilsson, Resnik, Rysanek, Windgassen VPO Böhm	LP: Historical Recording Enterprises CD: Legato SRO 833

Die Frau ohne Schatten

Vienna
November–
December
1955

Role of Watchman
Rysanek, Goltz,
Höngen, Hopf,
Schöffler, Böhme
Vienna Opera Chorus
VPO
Böhm

LP: Decca LXT 5180-5184/GOM 554-557/
GOS 554-557
CD: Decca 425 9812

Der Rosenkavalier

London
December
1956

Roles of Faninal,
Footman & Waiter
Schwarzkopf,
Stich-Randall,
C.Ludwig, Gedda,
Edelmann
Chorus
Philharmonia
Karajan

LP: Columbia 33CX 1492-1495/
SAX 2269-2272
LP: Columbia (Germany) C 90566-90569/
STC 90566-90569
LP: Angel 3563
LP: EMI 1C 191 00459-00462/SLS 810/
EX 29 00453
CD: EMI CDS 749 3548/CDS 556 1132
Excerpts
LP: Columbia 33CX 1777/SAX 2423
LP: Columbia (Germany) C 80661/STC 80661
LP: EMI 1C 063 00720
CD: EMI CDM 763 4522/CDCFP 4656/
CZS 252 1592

Salome

Vienna
October
1961

Role of Jochanaan
Nilsson,
G.Hoffman,
Stolze, Kmennt
VPO
Solti

LP: Decca MET 228-229/SET 228-229
CD: Decca 414 4142

Heimliche Aufforderung (Auf, hebe die funkelnde Schale!)

Vienna	H.Schmidt	LP: Amadeo AVRS 6257
1957		CD: Sony (Austria) 471 9112

Morgen (Und morgen wird die Sonne wieder scheinen)

Vienna	H.Schmidt	LP: Amadeo AVRS 6257
1957		CD: Sony (Austria) 471 9112

Die Nacht (Aus dem Walde tritt die Nacht)

Vienna	H.Schmidt	LP: Amadeo AVRS 6257
1957		CD: Sony (Austria) 471 9112

Traum durch die Dämmerung (Weite Wiesen im Dämmergrau)

Vienna	H.Schmidt	LP: Amadeo AVRS 6257
1957		CD: Sony (Austria) 471 9112

Zueignung (Ja, du weisst es, teure Seele!)

Vienna	H.Schmidt	LP: Amadeo AVRS 6257
1957		CD: Sony (Austria) 471 9112

IGOR STRAVINSKY (1882–1971)

Les noces

Vienna	Steingruber,	LP: Vanguard PVL 7009
1953	Kenny, Wagner	
	Kammerchor	
	Instrumentalists	
	Rossi	

Canticum sacrum

Cologne	Holm	Unpublished radio broadcast
February	WDR Orchestra	
1957	and Chorus	
	Rosbaud	

GIUSEPPE VERDI (1813-1901)

Un ballo in maschera, Querschnitt

Berlin 1965	Role of Renato Hillebrecht, Otto, Töpper, Schock Deutsche Oper Orchestra Hollreiser Sung in German	LP: Eurodisc KR 86812/XB 25968/XF 88047/ KR 72614/KR 72615/200.417 241/ 201.593 250/300.645 370

Don Carlos

Vienna October 1970	Role of Posa Janowitz, Verrett, Corelli, Ghiaurov, Talvela Vienna Opera Chorus VPO Stein	LP: Morgan MOR 7003 LP: Legendary Recordings LR 163 CD: Legato SRO 514 CD: Rodolphe RPC 32653-32655 CD: Panthéon PHC 6614-6616

Rigoletto, Querschnitt

Cologne 1963	Role of Rigoletto Hollweg, Konya WDR Orchestra Marszalek Sung in German	LP: Polydor LPHM 46 652/SLPHM 237 152

Simone Boccanegra

Vienna March 1969	Role of Boccanegra Janowitz, Cossutta, Kerns, Ghiaurov Vienna Opera Chorus VPO Krips	Unpublished radio broadcast Excerpts CD: Legato SRO 514

Il trovatore, Querschnitt

Cologne 1963	Role of Luna Hillebrecht, Malaniuk, Konya WDR Orchestra Marszalek Sung in German	LP: Polydor LPHM 46 652/SLPHM 237 152
Berlin 1965	Hillebrecht, Schock Deutsche Oper Orchestra Hollreiser Sung in German	LP: Eurodisc XB 25968/XF 79915/KR 72614/ KR 72615/200.417 241/300.645 370

RICHARD WAGNER (1813-1883)

Lohengrin

Bayreuth July 1958	Role of Heerrufer Rysanek, Varnay, Konya, Blanc, Engen Bayreuth Festival Orchestra & Chorus Cluytens	LP: Replica RPL 2489-2492 CD: Myto MCD 89062
Bayreuth July 1959	Grümmer, Gorr, Konya, Blanc, Crass Bayreuth Festival Orchestra & Chorus Matacic	LP: Melodram MEL 591
Bayreuth August 1960	Nordmo-Lövberg, Varnay, Adam, Windgassen, Neidlinger Bayreuth Festival Orchestra & Chorus Maazel	LP: Melodram MEL 601

Die Meistersinger von Nürnberg

Bayreuth   Role of Kothner   LP: Melodram MEL 582
July 1958   Grümmer, Schärtel,
                Traxel, Stolze,
                Wiener, Hotter,
                Blankenheim
                Bayreuth Festival
                Orchestra & Chorus
                Cluytens

Bayreuth   Grümmer, Schärtel,   LP: Melodram MEL 592
July 1959   Schock, Stolze,
                Wiener, Greindl,
                Blankenheim
                Bayreuth Festival
                Orchestra & Chorus
                Leinsdorf

Parsifal

Bayreuth   Role of Amfortas   LP: Melodram MEL 583
July 1958   Crespin, Beirer,
                Hines, Greindl,
                Blankenheim
                Bayreuth Festival
                Orchestra & Chorus
                Knappertsbusch

Bayreuth   Mödl, Beirer,   Unpublished radio broadcast
August   Hines, Greindl,   Opening up to Recht so! Habt Dank!
1959   Blankenheim   CD: Hunt CDKAR 219
                Bayreuth Festival   Incorrectly described as Vienna 1961
                Orchestra & Chorus
                Knappertsbusch

Vienna   C.Ludwig, Höngen,   CD: Hunt CDKAR 219
April 1961   Uhl, Hotter,   Opening of performance, up to and
                Franc, Berry   including first scene with Amfortas,
                Vienna Opera Chorus   taken from Bayreuth 1959 performance
                VPO   listed above
                Karajan

Das Rheingold

Vienna
September–
October
1958
	Role of Donner
	Flagstad, Watson,
	Madeira, Kuen,
	Kmennt, Svanholm,
	Neidlinger, London,
	Kreppel, Böhme
	VPO
	Solti
		LP: Decca LXT 5495-5497/SXL 2101-2103/
		    SET 382-384/D100 D19/RING 1-22/
		    414 1011/414 1001
		CD: Decca 414 1012/414 1002/455 5552
		Excerpts
		45: Decca CEP 632/SEC 5042
		LP: Decca LXT 5586/SXL 2230
		CD: Decca 421 3132

Tannhäuser

Rome November 1957	Role of Wolfram Brouwenstijn, Wilfert, Liebl, Pernerstorfer, Ernster RAI Roma Orchestra & Chorus Rodzinski	LP: Melodram MEL 472 CD: Datum 12318 Excerpts CD: Myto MCD 93277

Bayreuth
July 1962
	Silja, Bumbry,
	Windgassen,
	Crass, Greindl
	Bayreuth Festival
	Orchestra & Chorus
	Sawallisch
		LP: Philips AL 3445-3447/SAL 3445-3447/
		    A835 178-835 180Y/6747 242/
		    6747 249/6770 026/6723 001
		CD: Philips 420 1222/434 4202/434 6072
		Excerpts
		LP: Philips 6527 108/412 0231
		CD: Philips 446 6202

Vienna January 1963	Brouwenstijn, C.Ludwig, Beirer, Frick, Franc Vienna Opera Chorus VPO Karajan	LP: Melodram MEL 427 CD: Nuova Era 6307-6309 CD: Hunt CDKAR 204

Tannhäuser, excerpt (Blick' ich umher in diesem edlen Kreise)

Bamberg February 1956	Bamberg SO Leitner	45: DG EPL 30 234 LP: DG LPEM 19 069 LP: Decca (USA) DL 9928 LP: Preiser PR 135 015

Tannhäuser, excerpt (O du mein holder Abendstern)

Bamberg February 1956	Bamberg SO Leitner	45: DG EPL 30 234 LP: DG LPEM 19 069 LP: Decca (USA) DL 9928 LP: Preiser PR 135 015

Tristan und Isolde

Bayreuth July 1962	Role of Kurwenal Nilsson, Meyer, Windgassen, Greindl Bayreuth Festival Orchestra & Chorus Böhm	LP: Melodram MEL 625

Bayreuth
July-
August
1966
	Nilsson, C.Ludwig,
	Windgassen, Talvela
	Bayreuth Festival
	Orchestra & Chorus
	Böhm
		LP: DG LPM 19 221-19 225/
		    SLPM 139 221-139 225/2713 001/
		    2740 144/415 3951
		LP: Philips 6747 243
		CD: DG 415 3952/419 8892
		Excerpts
		LP: DG SLPEM 136 433/2537 001
		CD: DG 439 4692
		Rehearsal extracts from Act 3
		LP: DG LPM 19 221-19 225/
		    SLPM 139 221-139 225/2713 001/
		    2740 144

Bayreuth August 1966	Nilsson, C.Ludwig, Windgassen, Talvela Bayreuth Festival Orchestra & Chorus Böhm	CD: Frequenz CML 3 CD: Movimento musica 051.051 Excerpts CD: Curcio-Hunt OPV 16

CARL MARIA VON WEBER (1786-1826)

Der Freischütz

Munich
December
1959
	Role of Ottokar
	Seefried, Streich,
	Holm, Böhme,
	Kreppel
	Bavarian Radio
	Orchestra & Chorus
	Jochum
		LP: DG LPM 18 639-18 640/
		    SLPM 138 639-138 640/2707 009/
		    2726 061
		CD: DG 439 7172
		Excerpts
		LP: DG LPEM 19 221/SLPEM 136 221
		CD: DG 423 8692

Vienna May 1972	Janowitz, Holm, King, Jungwirth, Ridderbusch Vienna Opera Chorus VPO Böhm	CD: Hunt CDMP 457 CD: Foyer 2CF-2059

HUGO WOLF (1860-1903)

Ach wie lang die Seele schlummert/Spanisches Liederbuch

Vienna April-May 1959	Werba	LP: DG LPM 18 591/SLPM 138 059

Alle gingen, Herz, zur Ruh'/Spanisches Liederbuch

Vienna April-May 1959	Werba	LP: DG LPM 18 591/SLPM 138 059

Die du Gott gebarst, du Reine/Spanisches Liederbuch

Vienna April-May 1959	Werba	LP: DG LPM 18 591/SLPM 138 059

Wolf Lieder/continued

Gebet/Mörike-Lieder (Herr, schicke was du willst!)

Vienna 1957	H.Schmidt	LP: Amadeo AVRS 6257 CD: Sony (Austria) 471 9112

Gesang Weylas/Mörike-Lieder (Du bist Orplid, mein Land)

Vienna 1957	H.Schmidt	LP: Amadeo AVRS 6257 CD: Sony (Austria) 471 9112

Herr, was trägt der Boden hier/Spanisches Liederbuch

Vienna April-May 1959	Seefried Werba	LP: DG LPM 18 591/SLPM 138 059

Komm', o Tod!/Spanisches Liederbuch

Vienna April-May 1959	Werba	LP: DG LPM 18 591/SLPM 138 059

Nun bin ich dein!/Spanisches Liederbuch

Vienna April-May 1959	Werba	LP: DG LPM 18 591/SLPM 138 059

Peregrina/Mörike-Lieder (Warum, Geliebte, denk' ich dein?)

Vienna 1957	H.Schmidt	LP: Amadeo AVRS 6257 CD: Sony (Austria) 471 9112

Sterb' ich, so hüllt in Blumen mich/Italienisches Liederbuch

Vienna 1957	H.Schmidt	LP: Amadeo AVRS 6257 CD: Sony (Austria) 471 9112

Wolf Lieder/concluded

Treibe nur mit Lieben Spott/Spanisches Liederbuch

Vienna April-May 1959	Werba	LP: DG LPM 18 591/SLPM 138 059

Und willst du deinen Liebsten sterben sehen/Italienisches Liederbuch

Vienna 1957	H.Schmidt	LP: Amadeo AVRS 6257 CD: Sony (Austria) 471 9112

Wenn du mich mit den Augen streifst/Italienisches Liederbuch

Vienna 1957	H.Schmidt	LP: Amadeo AVRS 6257 CD: Sony (Austria) 471 9112

Wer sein holdes Lieb verloren/Spanisches Liederbuch

Vienna April-May 1959	Werba	LP: DG LPM 18 591/SLPM 138 059

Wunden trägst du, mein Geliebter/Spanisches Liederbuch

Vienna April-May 1959	Seefried Werba	LP: DG LPM 18 591/SLPM 138 059

CARL ZELLER (1842-1898)

Der Vogelhändler, Querschnitt

Vienna 1956	Role of Würmchen Zadek, Lipp, Patzak, Preger Vienna Opera Chorus VSO Moralt	LP: Philips S04031L/P08485L/P14706L/ SBL 5215/695 100KL

Discographies

Teachers and pupils
Schwarzkopf / Ivogün / Cebotari /
Seinemeyer / Welitsch / Streich / Berger
7 separate discographies, 400 pages

The post-war German tradition
Kempe / Keilberth / Sawallisch /Kubelik /
Cluytens
5 separate discographies, 300 pages

**Mid-century conductors
and More Viennese singers**
Böhm / De Sabata / Knappertsbusch / Serafin /
Krauss / Dermota / Rysanek / Wächter /
Reining / Kunz
10 separate discographies, 420 pages

Leopold Stokowski
Discography and concert register, 300 pages

Tenors in a lyric tradition
Fritz Wunderlich / Walther Ludwig /
Peter Anders
3 separate discographies, 350 pages

Makers of the Philharmonia
Galliera / Susskind / Kletzki / Malko / Matacic /
Dobrowen / Kurtz / Fistoulari
8 separate discographies, 300 pages

A notable quartet
Janowitz / Ludwig / Gedda / Fischer-Dieskau
4 separate discographies, 600 pages

Hungarians in exile
Reiner / Dorati /Szell
3 separate discographies, 300 pages

The art of the diva
Muzio / Callas / Olivero
3 separate discographies, 225 pages

The lyric baritone
Reinmar / Hüsch / Metternich / Uhde /
Wächter
5 separate discographies, 225 pages

Price £22 per volume (£28 outside UK)
*Special offer any 3 volumes for
£55 (£75 outside UK)*
Postage included
Order from: John Hunt, Flat 6,
37 Chester Way, London SE11 4UR

Credits

Valuable help with the supply of
information or illustration material
for these discographies came from:

John Ardoin, Dallas
Mike Ashman, Ware
Ray Burford, Sony Classical London
Richard Chlupaty, London
Clifford Elkin, Glasgow
Bill Flowers, London
Michael Gray, Alexandria VA
Syd Gray, Hove
Paul Gunther, Minnesota Orchestra
Bill Holland, Polygram London
Ken Jagger, EMI Classics London
Roderick Krüsemann, Amsterdam
Luis Luna, Berlin
Alan Newcombe, DG Hamburg
John Raymon, London
Phil Rees, Pewsey
Malcolm Walker, Harrow

Discographies by Travis & Emery:

Discographies by John Hunt.

1987: 978-1-906857-14-1: From Adam to Webern: the Recordings of von Karajan.
1991: 978-0-951026-83-0: 3 Italian Conductors and 7 Viennese Sopranos: 10 Discographies: Arturo Toscanini, Guido Cantelli, Carlo Maria Giulini, Elisabeth Schwarzkopf, Irmgard Seefried, Elisabeth Gruemmer, Sena Jurinac, Hilde Gueden, Lisa Della Casa, Rita Streich.
1992: 978-0-951026-85-4: Mid-Century Conductors and More Viennese Singers: 10 Discographies: Karl Boehm, Victor De Sabata, Hans Knappertsbusch, Tullio Serafin, Clemens Krauss, Anton Dermota, Leonie Rysanek, Eberhard Waechter, Maria Reining, Erich Kunz.
1993: 978-0-951026-87-8: More 20th Century Conductors: 7 Discographies: Eugen Jochum, Ferenc Fricsay, Carl Schuricht, Felix Weingartner, Josef Krips, Otto Klemperer, Erich Kleiber.
1994: 978-0-951026-88-5: Giants of the Keyboard: 6 Discographies: Wilhelm Kempff, Walter Gieseking, Edwin Fischer, Clara Haskil, Wilhelm Backhaus, Artur Schnabel.
1994: 978-0-951026-89-2: Six Wagnerian Sopranos: 6 Discographies: Frieda Leider, Kirsten Flagstad, Astrid Varnay, Martha Moedl, Birgit Nilsson, Gwyneth Jones.
1995: 978-0-952582-70-0: Musical Knights: 6 Discographies: Henry Wood, Thomas Beecham, Adrian Boult, John Barbirolli, Reginald Goodall, Malcolm Sargent.
1995: 978-0-952582-71-7: A Notable Quartet: 4 Discographies: Gundula Janowitz, Christa Ludwig, Nicolai Gedda, Dietrich Fischer-Dieskau.
1996: 978-0-952582-72-4: The Post-War German Tradition: 5 Discographies: Rudolf Kempe, Joseph Keilberth, Wolfgang Sawallisch, Rafael Kubelik, Andre Cluytens.
1996: 978-0-952582-73-1: Teachers and Pupils: 7 Discographies: Elisabeth Schwarzkopf, Maria Ivoguen, Maria Cebotari, Meta Seinemeyer, Ljuba Welitsch, Rita Streich, Erna Berger.
1996: 978-0-952582-77-9: Tenors in a Lyric Tradition: 3 Discographies: Peter Anders, Walther Ludwig, Fritz Wunderlich.
1997: 978-0-952582-78-6: The Lyric Baritone: 5 Discographies: Hans Reinmar, Gerhard Huesch, Josef Metternich, Hermann Uhde, Eberhard Waechter.
1997: 978-0-952582-79-3: Hungarians in Exile: 3 Discographies: Fritz Reiner, Antal Dorati, George Szell.
1997: 978-1-901395-00-6: The Art of the Diva: 3 Discographies: Claudia Muzio, Maria Callas, Magda Olivero.
1997: 978-1-901395-01-3: Metropolitan Sopranos: 4 Discographies: Rosa Ponselle, Eleanor Steber, Zinka Milanov, Leontyne Price.
1997: 978-1-901395-02-0: Back From The Shadows: 4 Discographies: Willem Mengelberg, Dimitri Mitropoulos, Hermann Abendroth, Eduard Van Beinum.
1997: 978-1-901395-03-7: More Musical Knights: 4 Discographies: Hamilton Harty, Charles Mackerras, Simon Rattle, John Pritchard.
1998: 978-1-901395-94-5: Conductors On The Yellow Label: 8 Discographies: Fritz Lehmann, Ferdinand Leitner, Ferenc Fricsay, Eugen Jochum, Leopold Ludwig, Artur Rother, Franz Konwitschny, Igor Markevitch.
1998: 978-1-901395-95-2: More Giants of the Keyboard: 5 Discographies: Claudio Arrau, Gyorgy Cziffra, Vladimir Horowitz, Dinu Lipatti, Artur Rubinstein.
1998: 978-1-901395-96-9: Mezzo and Contraltos: 5 Discographies: Janet Baker, Margarete Klose, Kathleen Ferrier, Giulietta Simionato, Elisabeth Hoengen.

1999: 978-1-901395-97-6: The Furtwaengler Sound Sixth Edition: Discography and Concert Listing.
1999: 978-1-901395-98-3: The Great Dictators: 3 Discographies: Evgeny Mravinsky, Artur Rodzinski, Sergiu Celibidache.
1999: 978-1-901395-99-0: Sviatoslav Richter: Pianist of the Century: Discography.
2000: 978-1-901395-04-4: Philharmonic Autocrat 1: Discography of: Herbert Von Karajan [Third Edition].
2000: 978-1-901395-05-1: Wiener Philharmoniker 1 - Vienna Philharmonic and Vienna State Opera Orchestras: Discography Part 1 1905-1954.
2000: 978-1-901395-06-8: Wiener Philharmoniker 2 - Vienna Philharmonic and Vienna State Opera Orchestras: Discography Part 2 1954-1989.
2001: 978-1-901395-07-5: Gramophone Stalwarts: 3 Separate Discographies: Bruno Walter, Erich Leinsdorf, Georg Solti.
2001: 978-1-901395-08-2: Singers of the Third Reich: 5 Discographies: Helge Roswaenge, Tiana Lemnitz, Franz Voelker, Maria Mueller, Max Lorenz.
2001: 978-1-901395-09-9: Philharmonic Autocrat 2: Concert Register of Herbert Von Karajan Second Edition.
2002: 978-1-901395-10-5: Sächsische Staatskapelle Dresden: Complete Discography.
2002: 978-1-901395-11-2: Carlo Maria Giulini: Discography and Concert Register.
2002: 978-1-901395-12-9: Pianists For The Connoisseur: 6 Discographies: Arturo Benedetti Michelangeli, Alfred Cortot, Alexis Weissenberg, Clifford Curzon, Solomon, Elly Ney.
2003: 978-1-901395-14-3: Singers on the Yellow Label: 7 Discographies: Maria Stader, Elfriede Troetschel, Annelies Kupper, Wolfgang Windgassen, Ernst Haefliger, Josef Greindl, Kim Borg.
2003: 978-1-901395-15-0: A Gallic Trio: 3 Discographies: Charles Muench, Paul Paray, Pierre Monteux.
2004: 978-1-901395-16-7: Antal Dorati 1906-1988: Discography and Concert Register.
2004: 978-1-901395-17-4: Columbia 33CX Label Discography.
2004: 978-1-901395-18-1: Great Violinists: 3 Discographies: David Oistrakh, Wolfgang Schneiderhan, Arthur Grumiaux.
2006: 978-1-901395-19-8: Leopold Stokowski: Second Edition of the Discography.
2006: 978-1-901395-20-4: Wagner Im Festspielhaus: Discography of the Bayreuth Festival.
2006: 978-1-901395-21-1: Her Master's Voice: Concert Register and Discography of Dame Elisabeth Schwarzkopf [Third Edition].
2007: 978-1-901395-22-8: Hans Knappertsbusch: Kna: Concert Register and Discography of Hans Knappertsbusch, 1888-1965. Second Edition.
2008: 978-1-901395-23-5: Philips Minigroove: Second Extended Version of the European Discography.
2009: 978-1-901395--24-2: American Classics: The Discographies of Leonard Bernstein and Eugene Ormandy.

Discography by Stephen J. Pettitt, edited by John Hunt:
1987: 978-1-906857-16-5: Philharmonia Orchestra: Complete Discography 1945-1987

Available from: Travis & Emery at 17 Cecil Court, London, UK.
(+44) 20 7 240 2129. email on sales@travis-and-emery.com .

© Travis & Emery 2009

Music and Books published by Travis & Emery Music Bookshop:
Anon.: Hymnarium Sarisburiense, cum Rubricis et Notis Musicis.
Agricola, Johann Friedrich from Tosi: Anleitung zur Singkunst.
Bach, C.P.E.: edited W. Emery: Nekrolog or Obituary Notice of J.S. Bach.
Bateson, Naomi Judith: Alcock of Salisbury
Bathe, William: A Briefe Introduction to the Skill of Song
Bax, Arnold: Symphony #5, Arranged for Piano Four Hands by Walter Emery
Burney, Charles: The Present State of Music in France and Italy
Burney, Charles: The Present State of Music in Germany, The Netherlands ...
Burney, Charles: An Account of the Musical Performances ... Handel
Burney, Karl: Nachricht von Georg Friedrich Handel's Lebensumstanden.
Cobbett, W.W.: Cobbett's Cyclopedic Survey of Chamber Music. (2 vols.)
Corrette, Michel: Le Maitre de Clavecin
Crimp, Bryan: Dear Mr. Rosenthal ... Dear Mr. Gaisberg ...
Crimp, Bryan: Solo: The Biography of Solomon
d'Indy, Vincent: Beethoven: Biographie Critique
d'Indy, Vincent: Beethoven: A Critical Biography
d'Indy, Vincent: César Franck (in French)
Frescobaldi, Girolamo: D'Arie Musicali per Cantarsi. Primo & Secondo Libro.
Geminiani, Francesco: The Art of Playing the Violin.
Handel; Purcell; Boyce; Geene et al: Calliope or English Harmony: Volume First.
Hawkins, John: A General History of the Science and Practice of Music (5 vols.)
Herbert-Caesari, Edgar: The Science and Sensations of Vocal Tone
Herbert-Caesari, Edgar: Vocal Truth
Hopkins and Rimboult: The Organ. Its History and Construction.
Hunt, John: Adam to Webern: the recordings of von Karajan
Isaacs, Lewis: Hänsel and Gretel. A Guide to Humperdinck's Opera.
Isaacs, Lewis: Königskinder (Royal Children) A Guide to Humperdinck's Opera.
Lacassagne, M. l'Abbé Joseph : Traité Général des élémens du Chant.
Lascelles (née Catley), Anne: The Life of Miss Anne Catley.
Mainwaring, John: Memoirs of the Life of the Late George Frederic Handel
Malcolm, Alexander: A Treaty of Music: Speculative, Practical and Historical
Marx, Adolph Bernhard: Die Kunst des Gesanges, Theoretisch-Practisch
May, Florence: The Life of Brahms
Mellers, Wilfrid: Angels of the Night: Popular Female Singers of Our Time
Mellers, Wilfrid: Bach and the Dance of God
Mellers, Wilfrid: Beethoven and the Voice of God

Travis & Emery Music Bookshop
17 Cecil Court, London, WC2N 4EZ, United Kingdom.
Tel. (+44) 20 7240 2129

Music and Books published by Travis & Emery Music Bookshop:
Mellers, Wilfrid: Caliban Reborn - Renewal in Twentieth Century Music
Mellers, Wilfrid: François Couperin and the French Classical Tradition
Mellers, Wilfrid: Harmonious Meeting
Mellers, Wilfrid: Le Jardin Retrouvé, The Music of Frederic Mompou
Mellers, Wilfrid: Music and Society, England and the European Tradition
Mellers, Wilfrid: Music in a New Found Land: ... ... American Music
Mellers, Wilfrid: Romanticism and the Twentieth Century (from 1800)
Mellers, Wilfrid: The Masks of Orpheus: ...... the Story of European Music.
Mellers, Wilfrid: The Sonata Principle (from c. 1750)
Mellers, Wilfrid: Vaughan Williams and the Vision of Albion
Panchianio, Cattuffio: Rutzvanscad Il Giovine
Pearce, Charles: Sims Reeves, Fifty Years of Music in England.
Playford, John: An Introduction to the Skill of Musick.
Purcell, Henry et al: Harmonia Sacra ... The First Book, (1726)
Purcell, Henry et al: Harmonia Sacra ... Book II (1726)
Quantz, Johann: Versuch einer Anweisung die Flöte traversiere zu spielen.
Rameau, Jean-Philippe: Code de Musique Pratique, ou Methodes.
Rastall, Richard: The Notation of Western Music.
Rimbault, Edward: The Pianoforte, Its Origins, Progress, and Construction.
Rousseau, Jean Jacques: Dictionnaire de Musique
Rubinstein, Anton : Guide to the proper use of the Pianoforte Pedals.
Sainsbury, John S.: Dictionary of Musicians. Vol. 1. (1825). 2 vols.
Simpson, Christopher: A Compendium of Practical Musick in Five Parts
Spohr, Louis: Autobiography
Spohr, Louis: Grand Violin School
Tans'ur, William: A New Musical Grammar; or The Harmonical Spectator
Terry, Charles Sanford: Four-Part Chorals of J.S. Bach. (German & English)
Terry, Charles Sanford: Joh. Seb. Bach, Cantata Texts, Sacred and Secular.
Terry, Charles Sanford: The Origins of the Family of Bach Musicians.
Tosi, Pierfrancesco: Opinioni de' Cantori Antichi, e Moderni
Van der Straeten, Edmund: History of the Violoncello, The Viol da Gamba ...
Van der Straeten, Edmund: History of the Violin, Its Ancestors... (2 vols.)
Walther, J. G.: Musicalisches Lexikon ober Musicalische Bibliothec

Travis & Emery Music Bookshop
17 Cecil Court, London, WC2N 4EZ, United Kingdom.
Tel. (+44) 20 7240 2129
© Travis & Emery 2009